DISCARDED

DOOMSDAY DELUSIONS

What's Wrong with Predictions About the End of the World

C. Marvin Pate & Calvin B. Haines Jr.

InterVarsity Press
Downers Grove, Illinois

InterVarsity Press® is the book-publishing division of InterVarsity Christian Fellowship®, a student movement active on campus at hundreds of universities, colleges and schools of nursing in the United States of America, and a member movement of the International Fellowship of Evangelical Students. For information about local and regional activities, write Public Relations Dept., InterVarsity Christian Fellowship, 6400 Schroeder Rd., P.O. Box 7895, Madison, WI 53707-7895.

Cover photograph: G. Brad Lewis/Tony Stone Images

ISBN 0-8308-1621-6

Printed in the United States of America

Library of Congress Cataloging-in-Publication Data

Pate, C. Marvin, 1952-
    Doomsday delusions: what's wrong with predictons about the end
    of the World/C. Marvin Pate and Calvin B. Haines, Jr.
        p.   cm.
    Includes bibliographical references.
    ISBN 0-8308-1621-6
    1. End of the world—Controversial literature. 2. Bible—
Prophecies—End of the world. 3. Bible—Criticism. interpretation,
etc. I. Haines, Calvin B. II. Title.
BT876.P38 1995
236'.9—dc20
                                              95-24330
                                                  CIP

20	19	18	17	16	15	14	13	12	11	10	9	8	7	6	5	4	3	2	1
12	11	10	09	08	07	06	05	04	03	02	01	00	99	98	97	96	95		

To Sheryl and Heather,
whose encouragement and insight helped
make this book possible.

C. M. P.

To Linda,
without whose love, patience,
encouragement and wisdom
I could not have completed this book.

C. B. H.

Acknowledgments

A book is the product of a joint effort, and this work is no exception. We sincerely wish to thank the following people for their indispensable assistance. We are grateful to Jim Hoover of InterVarsity Press, who not only worked with us to shape the book, but also helped us to attend to all the details that are inherent in such a project. We also wish to thank our assistants, Cathy Wegner and Ryan Hannah, whose typing and clerical skills were superior and invaluable. Finally, we want to express our appreciation to our families, colleagues and students, whose insights helped to refine this book.

Preface

Just after noon on April 19, 1993, smoke began billowing from windows in a Branch Davidian cult compound in Waco, Texas. The group inside, led by self-proclaimed messiah David Koresh, had been engaged in a standoff with federal authorities for fifty-one days. On February 28, as government agents tried to serve arrest warrants for possession of illegal weapons to those in the compound, a forty-five-minute gun battle broke out. By the time the smoke had cleared, four of the agents and one cult member were dead. Throughout the siege, Koresh claimed the confrontation was fulfilling his prophecy that he, as the messiah, would be persecuted.[1]

The authorities wanted to bring the long impasse to an end. To force Koresh to negotiate, early on the morning of April 19 tanklike vehicles were sent in to ram holes in the compound's buildings and shoot nonlethal tear gas inside. Cult members fired on the vehicles, but there was no other response until noon. At that time smoke appeared in the windows of the compound. Later, FBI officials said that two fires erupted at the same time after cult members spread a liquid, probably an accelerant, and ignited it. With strong winds blowing across the prairie, the entire compound was consumed by fire and completely leveled in less than half an hour. The federal agents had no idea that Koresh would end the standoff in this manner and were taken completely by surprise. Senior FBI agent Bob A. Ricks told reporters, "I can't tell you the shock and the horror that all of us felt when we saw those flames coming out of there. It was, 'Oh, my God, they're killing themselves.' "[2]

On that day Koresh and seventy-five to eighty-five of the Branch

Davidians, including more than twenty children, were burned to death, some beyond recognition. What would lead these people to allow themselves to be consumed by fire, to sacrifice their lives and those of their children in such a seemingly meaningless way? Why didn't more than a few escape when they could? Why did Koresh wait almost six hours after the tanks were sent in to set the fires? The answer lies in the cult's eschatology, that is, their understanding of the end times. An examination of Koresh's apocalyptic teachings makes it clear that what happened on April 19 was no surprise at all. The Branch Davidians in Waco had become obsessed with the Second Coming of Jesus Christ. Koresh proclaimed that he himself was Christ and that he was about to judge his enemies. The judgment would come through fire. Koresh twisted a number of biblical prophetic passages and taught that his adversaries would attack the compound but would be engulfed in a great apocalyptic inferno. The cult members would be taken in the blaze also, but they would be purified by the fire, while their foes would be destroyed.[3]

It is easy to feel great pity for those who got caught up in the deceit of the charismatic Koresh, but we might tend to think that they were, after all, neurotically preoccupied with the Second Coming and that such events are isolated incidents, unlikely to occur again soon. It is assumed that such a thing could never happen to rational, mainstream believers. After all, the Branch Davidians were a cultic offshoot of a denomination that began as a sect, the Seventh-day Adventists.

What many do not realize is that similar aberrant behavior is on the rise and, we believe, will intensify as the year 2000 approaches. In 1990, Elizabeth Clare Prophet, a New Age guru who claims she can communicate directly with Jesus and Buddha, called her flock in the Church Universal and Triumphant to its thirty-three-thousand-acre spread in Montana to prepare for the coming Armageddon. Thousands of the cult's members sold their possessions and moved to Paradise Valley, where they have built numerous bomb shelters, stockpiled weapons, and hoarded provisions and medical supplies in anticipation of the imminent end. Ironically, Prophet predicted that a nuclear holocaust would soon follow because political relations between the

United States and the Soviet Union were getting *better.* Prophet's technique for dealing with failed prophecies, including one in 1987 in which she said California would drop off into the sea, is to claim that her prayers and those of her followers delayed the predicted disasters.[4]

On the night of October 28, 1992, some fifteen hundred riot police and numerous ambulances and other emergency vehicles waited outside the Dami Missionary Church in Seoul, South Korea. They were anticipating the desperate frenzy that might occur when those inside the church were not taken up to heaven as they thought they would be. More than one thousand Dami members were inside awaiting the *hyoo-go,* or rapture of believers, that their leader, Lee Jang Rim, had predicted would occur on that night. Members of the church had ignited a widespread panic in South Korea and in certain parts of the United States as many of them sold their belongings and resigned from their jobs; four of them even committed suicide. After the prophecy failed, irate members of the church physically attacked those responsible for the prediction. In September 1992, Lee had been arrested for fleecing his flock of hundreds of thousands of dollars. When his prediction did not come true he also faced fraud charges. The only explanation offered for this phenomenon was that many South Koreans had been disturbed by the turbulent economic and political state of their country and perhaps believed the end was near.[5]

In 1992 Harold Camping, who owns a large network of Christian radio stations in the United States, announced his prediction that Christ would return between September 15 and 27, 1994. For two years he broadcast his predictions internationally on his radio talk show. He also published two books that detailed his views. Camping's following was so strong that he was able to found his own church, and donations to his radio network increased dramatically. When the September 27, 1994, deadline passed, Camping did not admit he was wrong but instead explained that he had merely miscalculated the biblical chronologies that were a large part of his theory.[6]

In October 1994, in Switzerland and Canada, fifty-three members of the Order of the Solar Temple, an apocalyptic cult, were killed or committed suicide, and the sites of these mass deaths were burned to the ground, presumably by other cult members. Some of the victims had been shot or had plastic bags tied over their heads, and their bodies were clothed in ceremonial robes and were found lying in a circle facing what appeared to be a chapel.[7]

Even more recently, another apocalyptic cult was blamed for a nerve gas attack on a Tokyo subway train in March 1995. Ten died in that incident and thousands were hospitalized as the poisonous sarin, developed by the Nazis in the 1930s, took its effect. The attack would have claimed even more lives if the gas had been distributed in a purer form. A few days after the subway incident, the police raided twenty-five branches of the cult held responsible, Aum Shinrikyo (Aum Supreme Truth), and discovered tons of chemicals that could be used for making nerve gas. Aum follows the syncretistic teachings of its founder, Shoko Asahara, a near-blind mystic. The cult has a substantial global outreach; for example, in Russia, where the group is especially popular, there are as many as 40,000 followers. Asahara, who originally combined elements of Buddhism, Hinduism and yoga to achieve inner enlightenment, has changed his views in recent years. He now focuses on an Armageddon-like scenario launched by the United States, which he says is run by Freemasons and Jews who want to destroy Japan. Asahara claims an assault has already begun with the increasingly overwhelming influence of the West and will culminate violently with the world's destruction, somewhere between 1997 and 2000. In fact, Aum's popularity in Japan has been attributed to the spiritual emptiness and disillusionment many young people experience in the midst of Western-style financial success and materialism. Potential members must survive a series of strenuous initiations, renounce all family connections and hand over their assets to the group. For what purpose? Asahara assures them that only his followers and a nominal number of those outside the Aum movement will survive the great final battle with the West. Asahara has been quoted as saying that such weapons as sarin must be used in times of emergency to kill one's enemies quickly and efficiently. It is numbing to think of the implications of an eschatology in which Armageddon is brought on through nerve gas terrorism.[8]

It needs to be noted that even though many mainstream believers claim that they would never engage in the kinds of behavior we have just described, many evangelicals have done such things in the past when they became fixated on the Second Coming. Further, we fear that certain evangelicals today, because of the way in which they interpret biblical prophetic passages, are setting themselves up for a similar fall. This may sound overly dramatic, but consider the following: A significant number of evangelicals interpret Scripture in such a way that they believe the beginning of the end of the world commenced in 1948 when Israel became a modern state. They are convinced that we are indeed living in the last generation before Christ's return. Since they believe we are definitely near the end, they see evidence for the Second Advent all around them, from the deterioration of morals in our society, to the tumultuous events on the global political scene, to the perceived increase in natural disasters. They then may very easily give in to the temptation of becoming prognosticators of the end times. Those who adhere to such a mindset have adopted what might be called the doomsday mentality. How might people behave if they get wrapped up in all of this? We believe they may become obsessed with the Second Coming, focusing all of their attention and energy on its culmination, becoming predisposed to act in abnormal and foolish ways and taking on heretical beliefs. The consequences for fixating on Christ's return can be severe.

This book analyzes the phenomenon we have just described. In chapter one, we show how those who adopt the doomsday mentality are grounded in a questionable approach to interpreting Scripture: they read current events back into the biblical text; that is, they observe what is going on around them and see how these things are fulfillments of biblical prophecy. This is done, however, at the risk of misinterpreting the biblical authors. Chapter two focuses on the fact that the signs of the times—that so many prognosticators believe are now being revealed to disclose the timing of the Second Coming—actually began in the first century A.D. with Jesus and his generation. An analysis of the manner in which doomsayers misinterpret key biblical prophetic texts in a way that reinforces their theological presuppositions is offered in chapter three.

The last two chapters discuss what might happen to people who become preoccupied with Christ's return. Chapter four examines the way in which those who are convinced we are living in the last generation may become exclusive in their beliefs and separate from their fellow believers. Chapter five addresses the possible consequences of separation: heretical practices and episodes in which people stay committed to beliefs that have been proven categorically false, a phenomenon known as cognitive dissonance. Both of these chapters focus on a nineteenth-century movement of evangelicals that was based on a prediction that Christ would return in 1844, a movement which attracted tens of thousands of followers but was decimated when the prediction was not fulfilled. In the conclusion, we offer what we believe to be the proper, and indeed wonderful, role of the anticipation of Christ's return in the life of the believer.

1

When Prophecy Fails

Doomsday Preaching &
the Question of Interpretation

IN THINKING ABOUT THE ALARMIST PREDICTIONS OF MODERN doomsday "prophets," one is reminded of one of Aesop's ancient stories, *The Shepherd Boy and the Wolf:*

A mischievous lad, who was set to mind some sheep, used, in jest, to cry "Wolf! Wolf!" When the people at work in the neighboring fields came running to the spot he would laugh at them for their pains. One day the wolf came in reality, and the boy this time called "Wolf! Wolf!" in earnest; but the men, having been so often deceived, disregarded his cries, and the sheep were left at the mercy of the wolf.[1]

The moral of the story for our day is clear: the more biblical doomsayers inaccurately predict the end of history, the less people will take their warnings seriously. And if false predictions persist into the twenty-first century, our world, to its great detriment, may lose interest altogether in the return of Christ.[2]

Not that setting dates for the end of the world based on a certain interpretation of the Bible is not appealing. It certainly is. Doomsday prophets abound, and their predictions will undoubtedly proliferate as the year A.D. 2000 approaches. Their books are selling into the millions, and their influence over people is astounding. Paul Boyer, professor of history at the University of Wisconsin, estimates that there are some eight million biblical prophecy buffs today.[3] Their message is captivating. With boldness and apparent precision, some of the more well-known contemporary religious prognosticators identify Russia (recent events having forced them to find a substitute for the Soviet Union, which no longer exists) with Gog and Magog (Ezek 38—39), Red China with the "kings from the East" (Rev 16:12-16) and the European Common Market with the "ten horns of the beast" (Rev 13:1-10). Capitalizing on the Bible's relevance to modern society, these people commonly equate the locusts of Revelation 9:7-10 with Cobra helicopters and their deadly sting with nerve gas sprayed from the chopper's tail, or associate credit cards with the mark of the beast (666) of Revelation 13.[4] Repeatedly these commentators of the modern era assert that we are living in the midst of the fulfillment of the signs of the times, as heralded by Jesus. Matthew 24:7 is seen to be fulfilled by famines like the ones in Ethiopia and Rwanda, earthquakes like those in California and Japan, and strife in the Middle East, Yugoslavia and Los Angeles. Who can resist the appeal of the headlines in prophecy books showcased in many Christian bookstores: "Babylon Rebuilt"; "Ark of the Covenant Discovered"; "The Computer Beast in Belgium"; "Is Gorbachev Gog?"; and "Is Carlos the Antichrist?"

Some of the prophets are downright funny—like the sincere doomsayer who observes that the false prophet who will make an image of the antichrist (Rev 13:14-15) will be better equipped to do so because of the development of robotics.[5] Or the author who firmly believes that the white horse of Revelation 6:2 is a symbol of the United States, because its flag colors are red, *white* and blue.[6] Then there is the prophecy fanatic who sent a letter to a minister announcing that the building blocks of the end-time Jewish temple have all been cut and numbered, and are presently being stored in Kmarts across the United States, awaiting the call to ship them to Jerusalem.[7]

However, the far-reaching ramifications of the power of doomsayers to bring about self-fulfilling prophecies is no laughing matter. The tragic end of self-proclaimed prophets like Jim Jones and David Koresh pales in significance compared to the global threat that could result from the wedding of contemporary prophetic crystal-ball readers and political theory. D. S. Russell, expert in Jewish-Christian apocalyptic literature, expresses it powerfully:

> One rather frightening by-product of this process of interpretation is that it is so easy to *create* the very situation which is being described so that the interpretation given brings about its own fulfilment. Russia, for example, is to be destroyed by nuclear attack—and scripture must be fulfilled! It needs little imagination to understand the consequences of such a belief, especially if held with deep conviction by politicians and the military who have the power to press the button and to execute the judgment thus prophesied and foreordained.[8]

The preceding caveat, however, should not be misread as an invective against biblical prophecy. The authors believe in the inspired nature of biblical prophecy, and later we will attempt to provide both a right understanding of and a proper response to it. Rather, what we call into question here is the *interpretation* of biblical prophecy by the typical doomsday prophet. In particular, those who set dates for the end of the world fail to properly understand the genre or literary form of eschatological ("end-time") prophecy as found in both scriptural and nonscriptural writings dating between 200 B.C. and A.D. 100. Accordingly, this chapter documents both a wrong way and a right way to handle such material. Three points will be addressed: (1) a history of failed doomsday prophecy; (2) a better approach to end-time prophecy; (3) how doomsday prophecy goes awry.

A History of Failed Doomsday Prophecy

"To prophesy," as the Chinese proverb puts it, "is extremely difficult—especially with respect to the future." The difficulty of prophesying is emphasized in the Old Testament. Deuteronomy 18:20-22 acknowledges the eventuality of failed prophecies, even of predictions made in the name of the Lord:

> But a prophet who presumes to speak in my name anything I have not commanded him to say, or a prophet who speaks in the name of other gods, must be put to death.
>
> You may say to yourselves, "How can we know when a message has not been spoken by the LORD?" If what a prophet proclaims in the name of the LORD does not take place or come true, that is a message the LORD has not spoken. That prophet has spoken presumptuously. Do not be afraid of him.

The threat of death for all who utter false predictions in the name óf the Lord aside, there are at least two points of application to today's doomsday prophets which we may draw from this text. First, such people presumptuously think they represent God. Second, such people are not sacrosanct; they need not terrify well-informed Christians with their alarmist warnings and empty promises. In any event, it is hard to place much confidence in today's prophetic seers who claim they know when Jesus will return when he himself does not: "No one knows about that day or hour, not even the angels in heaven, nor the Son, but only the Father" (Mk 13:32).

Tempting as it may be to identify Cobra helicopters with the locusts of Revelation 9 or to discover modern-day countries in ancient biblical prophecies, reading current events back into the prophetic text is a bad method of scriptural interpretation. We can learn how inappropriate it is by looking back in history at some rather famous examples of this approach.

Predicting the end of the world is not the prerogative of Christian preachers; some ancient Jewish theologians did the same. Josephus, a first-century A.D. Jewish historian, documents a number of instances related to prophetic phenomena during the late Second Temple Period (c. A.D. 40-72). Two in particular call for comment. First, Josephus reports the revolt of Theudas (c. A.D. 44-46; see *Antiquities of the Jews* 20.97-98; compare also Acts 5:36), who tried to lead a band of four hundred followers over the Jordan River in an apparent attempt to duplicate the miracle of Joshua (Josh 3). However, Theudas and his followers were killed by the Romans. David E. Aune makes some significant observations about the incident: (1) Theudas considered himself to be an eschatological prophet (2) who combined the claim to predict the future with the claim to be a miracle worker causing the parting of the Jordan River (3) in hopes of expelling the Romans from Palestine.[9]

Second, Josephus recounts an incident that occurred during the last days of the siege of Jerusalem by the Roman army, in August-September of A.D. 70. Six thousand Jews inside the city who took refuge in one of the porticoes of the temple were tragically incinerated when the building was set on fire by the Romans. Josephus explains the cause of the Jews' frantic activity and fiery demise: "A false prophet was the occasion of these people's destruction, who had made a public proclamation in the city that very day, that God commanded them to get up upon the temple, and that there they should receive miraculous signs of their deliverance" (*Jewish Wars* 6.285).

In tracking failed prophecies of doomsday preachers we fast forward through time to New Year's Eve, A.D. 999. Pope Sylvester II celebrated what he and many of the faithful thought would be the last midnight mass of history. Believing that, based on Revelation 20:7-8, the end of the world would occur when Satan was unleashed one thousand years after Christ's birth, they prepared for the final hour. Russell Chandler's encapsulation of the moment merits quoting in full:

> This was the final hour, the beginning of the day of wrath, the "nightfall of the universe," that fateful and dreaded eve of the turn of the millennium, when the earth would dissolve into ashes.
>
> Outside, anxious crowds flooded the streets. Church bells rang out what most thought would not be a new year but history's finale. And in Jerusalem, thousands of pilgrims milled about hysterically, flocking to the spot where they expected Jesus to descend from the clouds. They, too, were waiting for the End.
>
> All across Europe people had donated land, homes, and goods to the poor in acts of contrition. Debts had been canceled, infideli-

ties confessed, wrongdoings forgiven. Businesses had been neglected, buildings allowed to fall into disrepair or even torn down, and fields left uncultivated. Many had freed farm animals and slaves to prepare for the Final Judgment. Beggars had been fed, prisoners released, and churches besieged by crowds seeking absolution. By December flagellants roamed the countryside, whipping one another in penitence and mortification. And at Christmastide, shops had given away food while merchants took no payment.

On New Year's Eve, as the fatal hour was about to strike in venerable St. Peter's, Pope Sylvester II raised his hands skyward. The crowd—many dressed in sackcloth and ashes—remained transfixed, scarcely daring to breathe. As one account has it, the giant clock ticking away the last minutes of the first millennium suddenly stopped. Not a few died from fright, giving up their ghosts then and there. But after an awful moment that seemed like eternity suspended, the clock resumed its countdown. Only the ominous tick, tock and the voice of the pope broke the deathly silence. Sylvester chanted the sacred Latin phrases, and at precisely midnight the bells atop the great tower began to peal wildly.

The *Te Deum* was sung. And no fire fell from heaven.[10]

In the pages of modern history, a number of doomsday prophets come to mind. One thinks, for example, of the American nineteenth-century Baptist preacher and forerunner of Seventh-day Adventism, William Miller. Miller believed he had cracked the code for determining the date of the return of Christ and the end of the world.

Through numerous calculations using biblical prophetic passages as his guide, Miller arrived at what he thought was the time when the world would end: between March 21, 1843, and March 21, 1844. When that prophecy failed, one of Miller's followers recalculated and offered a revised date for the Second Advent, October 21, 1844.[11] It is amazing that despite the failure of Miller's predictions his disciples continued to follow him and hold him in high regard. We will see the reason for their—and others'—loyalty in a later chapter.

The twentieth century has witnessed an increase in the numbers of prophetic prognosticators, four of whom have recently captured the public's attention. Edgar C. Whisenant, in his book *88 Reasons Why the Rapture Will Be in 1988,*[12] predicted the return of Christ would take place in September 1988. When that event did not occur, he published a revised edition of his predictions in which he reset the date for the end of the world for October 3, 1989.[13] We have already discussed the chilling effects in South Korea as well as the United States of Lee Jang Rim's predictions that the rapture would take place in October 1992, and we know all too well the results of David Koresh's false prophecies. In the evangelical camp, Harold Camping's foretellings should also be added to the list of failed prophecies; his widely publicized prediction that Christ would return in September 1994 obviously did not materialize.

These prognosticators clearly set specific dates for the end of the world or offered scenarios that definitively outlined how the end would unfold.

Some of the apocalyptic writers of our time, however, have been much more careful and responsible with their handling of prophetic Scriptures than those just mentioned. Nevertheless, their interpretive techniques run the risk of paving the way for bizarre and blatant end-time forecastings. Couching their statements with hedges like "suggest," "could" and "probable," these theologians implicitly set the date of the return of Christ around the year A.D. 2000. All too often they assert that, with the formation of the nation of Israel in 1948, the end-time generation began. Thus, according to their prophetic calendar, the people of today's generation are the fulfillment of Mark 13:30, "This generation will certainly not pass away until all these things have happened" (compare Mt 24:34 and Lk 21:32).

A similar end-time scenario is espoused by many of these implicit date-setters. After a secret rapture of the church to heaven (1 Thess 4:13-18), a seven-year period of Great Tribulation will engulf the earth (Mt 24/Mk 13/Lk 21; Rev 6—19). This relatively short period will be precipitated by the rise of the antichrist, who, having made a peace pact with Israel, will then break that covenant and unleash a time of great persecution on the Jews, the people of God (Dan 9:24-27). He will lead a ten-nation European confederation against Israel (Dan 7;

Rev 17), but he will be opposed by an innumerable army from China, which will be following its own agenda for conquering the nations (Rev 9:16). Consequently, the world powers will meet head-on in the Valley of Armageddon (Rev 16:16). But at the climax of that battle, Christ will return a second time, in power and great glory, armed with the purpose of judging the godless nations (Zech 14:4; Rev 19:20). This he will do with fearsome authority, after which he will set up his earthly thousand-year kingdom in Jerusalem (Rev 20:1-6). However, at the end of that utopian period Satan will be permitted a brief reprisal of his evil role, after which he will be forever banished (Rev 20:7-10). Then comes the new Jerusalem and the eternal bliss of God's unhindered reign over the universe (Rev 21—22).

We have no quarrel with the broad contours of this eschatological landscape. We believe a good case can be made for the premillennial scenario the preceding apocalyptic drama presupposes, including the rise of the antichrist, the tribulation period, the cosmic catastrophes, the Second Coming of Christ, his thousand-year reign on earth and eternal punishment. These "signs of the times" were commonplaces found in both Jewish and Christian literature dating between 200 B.C. and A.D. 100. Our point of contention lies in anachronistically viewing current events as the necessary fulfillment of those end-time prophecies.[14] In our estimation, the basic flaw of the doomsday prophet is hermeneutical—though sincerely motivated, such a person allegorizes Scripture. This is the wrong way to handle biblical prophecy. The right way to handle that material is to interpret it within the context of its day—from a historical, cultural, grammatical and theological perspective.

A Better Approach to End-Time Prophecy

There is a right approach to biblical prophecy, and it begins with understanding its genre or literary pattern. Called by some "prophetic-apocalyptic"[15] and by others "eschatological prophecy"[16] (there is no substantial difference between the names), biblical prophecy fits into a type of literature dating between 200 B.C. and A.D. 100 (though it is not restricted to that time frame), whose provenance was in and around ancient Palestine. D. S. Russell provides a convenient list of Jewish apocalyptic literature dating from this time period (though we disagree with his dating of Daniel in particular): Daniel (165 B.C.); *1 Enoch* (c. 164 B.C.); *Jubilees* (c. 150 B.C.); *Sibylline Oracles,* book 3 (from c. 150 B.C. onwards); *Testaments of the Twelve Patriarchs* (latter part of second century B.C.); *Psalms of Solomon* (c. 48 B.C.); *Assumption of Moses* (A.D. 6-30); *Martyrdom of Isaiah; Life of Adam and Eve* or *Apocalypse of Moses* (shortly before A.D. 70); *Apocalypse of Abraham* 9—32 (c. A.D. 70-100); *Testament of Abraham* (first century A.D.); *2 Enoch* or *Book of the Secrets of Enoch* (first century A.D.); *Sibylline Oracles,* book 4 (c. A.D. 80); *2 Esdras* or *4 Ezra* 3—14 (c. A.D. 90); *2 Apocalypse of Baruch* (after A.D. 90); *3 Apocalypse of Baruch* (second century A.D.); *Sibylline Oracles,* book 5 (second century A.D.).[17]

Russell rightly also includes in this genre materials from the Dead Sea Scrolls discovered at Qumran (dating between 150 B.C. and A.D. 70): commentaries on Isaiah, Hosea, Micah, Nahum, Habakkuk, Zephaniah and Psalm 37; the *Zadokite Document* (or the *Damascus Document);* the *Manual of Discipline* (or the *Rule of the Community);* the *Rule of the Congregation;* a *Scroll of Benedictions;* the *Testimonies Scroll* (or a *Messianic Anthology); Hymns (*or *Psalms) of Thanksgiving;* the *War of the Sons of Light Against the Sons of Darkness* (or the *Rule for the Final War);* the *Book of Mysteries;* a *Midrash on the Last Days;* a *Description of the New Jerusalem;* an *Angelic Liturgy;* the *Prayer of Nabonidus;* a *Pseudo-Daniel Apocalypse;* and a *Genesis Apocryphon.*[18]

In addition to the noncanonical (nonscriptural) books listed, one could add Ezekiel 38—39 (c. 550 B.C.), which is very similar in genre to the biblical book of Daniel (c. 550 B.C.), as well as the following New Testament passages: Mark 13 (compare Mt 24; Lk 21); 2 Thessalonians 2; Revelation 6—19. To grasp the nature of this literature is to enable one to properly interpret it, the Scriptures included. By way of an overview of this subject, two points are covered here: the characteristics of end-time prophetic material and the interpretation of that literature.

The Characteristics of End-Time Prophetic Material

This literature is actually composed of a mixture of two literary genres—apocalyptic and prophecy. *Apocalyptic* is a word derived from the Greek word *apokalypsis* (the title of the New Testament book Revelation), which means "revelation" or "unveiling." The primary focus of this literature is the revelation of the events of the end of time. Leon Morris describes certain features shared by these works:

1. The writer tends to choose some great man of the past (for example, Enoch or Moses) and make him the hero of the book.

2. This hero often takes a journey accompanied by a celestial guide, who shows him interesting sights and comments on them.

3. Information is often communicated through visions.

4. The visions often make use of strange, even enigmatic, symbolism.

5. The visions often are pessimistic with regard to the possibility that human intervention will ameliorate the present situation.

6. The visions usually end with God bringing the present state of affairs to a cataclysmic end and establishing his kingdom.

7. The apocalyptic writer often uses a pseudonym, claiming to write in the name of his chosen hero.

8. The writer often takes past history and rewrites it as if it were prophecy.

9. The focus of apocalyptic is on comforting and sustaining the righteous remnant.[19]

George Ladd sees the development of apocalyptic as resulting from three main factors:

The first is the emergence of a Righteous Remnant, a minority group, usually without substantial political power, who view themselves as remaining faithful to God while surrounded by those who are not. A second factor is the problem of evil. As early as the Book of Job, the conception that God rewards the just and punishes evildoers had been recorded. How then could the Righteous Remnant reconcile the fact that they were oppressed by those much more wicked than themselves? Third, the cessation of prophecy (recorded in the noncanonical *2 Apocalypse of Baruch* 85:3) created a spiritual vacuum: the Righteous Remnant longed for a word from God but none was forthcoming. The apocalyptists attempted to bring a word of comfort and reassurance from God to the men of their day.[20]

A careful examination of the biblical texts previously listed (Ezek 38—39; Daniel; Mk 13/Mt 24/Lk 21; 2 Thess 2; Rev 6—19) will show that they possess a number of features characteristic of apocalyptic literature, especially items 2-6 and 9.[21]

A second genre, however, is apparent in the canonical works cited—prophecy, a brief overview of which we provide here. The major term for the Old Testament prophets is *nābî'*, which etymologically means "one who is called." Practically, however, the word came to mean "spokesman for God." There were various types of Old Testament prophets. First there were the shamanistic, or charismatic, prophets, like Samuel, Elijah and Elisha. Then there were the cult and temple prophets, like Ezekiel and Jeremiah. Ahab and Jezebel had court prophets. Amos, Hosea, Micah and Isaiah were free or independent prophets. The role of the Old Testament prophet was basically twofold: forthtelling and foretelling. Concerning the former aspect, the prophet declared God's word for his day which, with respect to the latter aspect, sometimes also involved distant fulfillment (e.g., Is 7:14; Ezek 38—39; Dan 9:24-27).

While the genre of prophecy is also present in the noncanonical literature listed earlier, it is accentuated in the biblical materials. Prophecy, though similar to apocalyptic literature (probably the latter developed out of the former), is distinguished from it in a number of ways. J. Barton Payne discusses those distinctions, which we summarize here:

1. The initial presentation of prophecy was usually in spoken form and was put in writing at a later time. The initial presentation of apocalyptic was usually in writing.

2. Prophetic utterances most often are separate, brief oracles. Apocalyptic utterances are often longer and more continuous; they have cycles of material repeated a second or third time in parallel form.

3. Apocalyptic tends to contain more symbolism, especially of animals and other living forms.

4. Apocalyptic places a greater stress on dualism (angels and the Messiah versus Satan and the antichrist) than does prophecy.

5. Apocalyptic primarily confirms and encourages the righteous remnant. Prophecy often castigates the nominally religious.

6. Apocalyptic is generally pessimistic about the effectiveness of human intervention in changing the present. Prophecy focuses on the importance of human change.

7. Apocalyptic was usually written pseudonymously. Prophecy was usually written or spoken in the name of its author.[22]

The above distinctions between prophecy and apocalyptic, however, are matters of degree and emphasis, rather than absolute differences. In fact the two genres share a number of significant similarities: both are concerned with the future; both frequently employ symbolic language to get their messages across; both emphasize the impact of the supernatural world on the natural world; both promise future redemption for the faithful believer.

The Interpretation of End-Time Prophetic Material

One reaches the crux of the matter with the question, How is end-time prophecy to be interpreted? The answer is that one should follow the standard fourfold procedure employed in the interpretation of the rest of the biblical materials, which is to look at the text historically, culturally, grammatically and theologically. Apart from the last criterion, this has been the normal approach to literature in general.

Approaching the Bible historically involves identifying the specific period in which the author lived. Who was he? To whom did he write? What is the purpose of the work? Particular historical situations inevitably colored the life setting of the author and his recipients. Many of the eschatological prophetic books can be dated to the postexilic period (the time when Israel returned to her land out of Babylonian captivity, 538 B.C. and following) and the Greco-Roman period (the time when the Greeks and the Romans occupied the land of Israel, c. 200 B.C. to A.D. 100). The biblical books, as we will see in chapter three of this work, allude to significant events occurring in these two historical periods (though they are not confined to these times; Daniel and Ezekiel were written during the time of the Baby-lonian captivity).

Knowing the cultural milieu of the biblical text greatly aids the modern reader's understanding of it. Geography, customs and norms contributed to the social environment of the writer. In particular, the clash of Judaism and Greco-Roman cultures resulted in the defeat and oppression of the Jewish people from 200 B.C. on, encompassing early Christianity as well. It was in the context of such oppression and persecution that eschatological prophecy flourished, for apocalyptic literature basically originates from a suffering minority.

Vital to interpreting the biblical text (as it is for grasping the meaning of any piece of literature) is a proper understanding of how the words in a sentence are related to one another (syntax). Henry Virkler provides a helpful sixfold grammatical procedure for accu-rately interpreting a biblical text: (1) identify the general literary form of the passage, whether prose, poetry or apocalyptic (the last of which may incorporate both the first two forms); (2) trace the development of the author's theme and show how the passage under consideration fits into the context; (3) identify the natural divisions of the text; (4) identify the connecting words within the paragraphs and sentences; (5) determine what the individual words mean; (6) analyze the syn-tax.[23]

With regard to the genre of end-time prophecy (which is rooted in apocalypticism), grasping the interplay between prose (which is to be interpreted literally) and poetry (which is to be interpreted symboli-cally) is essential to accurately understanding it. Of course, even prose may contain nonliteral elements, such as parables, allegories and figures of speech. But it is in the failure to grasp the interplay between prose and poetry that doomsday prophets make a major mistake, overemphasizing the literal meaning to the neglect of the symbolic. Both angles are important, and the proper relationship between them is best accounted for by *beginning* with the figurative meaning, behind which lies the literal reality. Put another way, end-time prophecy, because it more often than not emerged from a persecuted minority, is a coded language in need of deciphering. The reason for the use of coded language is obvious—it protected both author and recipients from the dominant, oppressing regimes of the day. Hence, for example, the prevalence of heavenly visions, enigmatic symbolism (for example, beasts representing political empires), gematria (figurative meaning attached to numbers such as 666), dualism (the clash of people groups described in terms of the struggle between supernatural powers). As such, eschatological prophecy's primary focus concerned the particular life setting of the biblical author and recipients, though its parameters also include the distant future.

The theological presuppositions of the author also require explanation. In studying end-time prophetic literature, the dominant theological motif contained therein is the Jewish doctrine of the two ages. According to early Judaism, time is divided into two consecutive periods—this age and the age to come. This age is characterized by sin and suffering as a result of Adam's fall. The age to come will be inaugurated when the Messiah comes and, with him, righteousness and peace. In effect, the age to come is synonymous with the kingdom of God. But according to the Gospels, the life, death and resurrection of Jesus Christ marked a paradigmatic shift resulting in the overlapping of the two ages. The age to come or the kingdom of God was inaugurated within this present age. In other words, the two ages overlap, and the Christian lives in the intersection of the two. This idea is commonly referred to as the "already/not yet" eschatological tension. That is, the age to come has "already" dawned because of the first coming of Christ, but is "not yet" complete; that awaits his second coming.

The overlapping of the two ages seems to have provided the theological stimulus for the mixing of the two genres inherent in eschatological prophecy, especially with regard to the New Testament. Accordingly, the prophetic side of the literature seems to be connected with the "already" aspect of the age to come, while the apocalyptic side seems to emphasize the "not yet" aspect of the age to come. The age to come has dawned within human history, but its consummation awaits the end of time. This tension between the two ages is foreshadowed in the Old Testament (e.g., Ezek 38—39; Dan 2, 7, 9:24-27) and approximated in Jewish intertestamental literature (e.g., the Dead Sea Scrolls), but it is only fully developed in the New Testament (e.g., Mk 13/Mt 24/Lk 21; 2 Thess 2; Rev 6—19). We will examine these passages in chapter two of this work, taking into consideration the historical, cultural, grammatical and theological principles (especially the last one mentioned). For the present purpose, however, we conclude this chapter by honing in on the twofold theological problem of the doomsday prophetic approach. That discussion will also pave the way for the next chapter.

How Doomsday Prophecy Goes Awry

There are two basic theological problems with the doomsday prophetic approach: (1) It overlooks the "already" aspect of end-time prophecy, the result of which is that it becomes obsessed with current events as the fulfillment of Scripture. That is, doomsday preachers do not focus on the *historical* fulfillment of prophetic Scriptures related to the first coming of Christ. (2) Consequently, doomsday preachers allegorize biblical prophecy, reading current events back into the text to make it relevant to their readers. This approach, not unlike the *pesher* technique prominent within the Qumran community of Jesus' day, is immediately appealing but is doomed to irrelevancy as the prophecies fail.

The "Already" Aspect of Biblical Prophecy

Simply put, modern-day doomsday prophets do not seem to realize that the first coming of Jesus Christ was imbued with eschatological significance. A generation ago, the British theologian C. H. Dodd rightly called attention to the early church's perspective on Jesus Messiah (especially as culled from the book of Acts). He noted that there were at least five end-time aspects of Jesus' life, death and resurrection. First, in Jesus the messianic age has dawned (Acts 2:16; 3:18, 24) in his ministry, death and resurrection (Acts 2:23). Second, by his resurrection, Jesus has been exalted to the right hand of God as messianic head of the new people of God (Acts 2:33-36; 3:13). Third, the Holy Spirit is the sign of the presence of the eschaton as well as the proof that Jesus currently reigns in heaven in power and glory (Acts 2:33). Fourth, the messianic age will shortly reach its consummation in the return of Christ (Acts 3:21). Fifth, an invitation is always extended for people to receive Christ and the life of the age to come (Acts 2:38-39).[24]

Gordon D. Fee captures the resulting eschatological tension that characterizes the Christian between the first and second comings of Jesus Christ:

> The absolutely essential framework of the self-understanding of primitive Christianity is an eschatological one. Christians had come to believe that, in the event of Christ, the new (coming) age had dawned, and that, especially through Christ's death and resurrection and the subsequent gift of the Spirit, God had set the future in motion, to be consummated by yet another coming (parousia) of Christ. Theirs was therefore an essentially eschatological existence. They lived "between the times" of the beginning and the consummation of the end. Already God had secured their . . . salvation; already they were the people of the future, living the life of the future in the present age—and enjoying its benefits. But they still awaited the glorious consummation of this salvation. Thus they lived in an essential tension between the "already" and the "not-yet."[25]

The first theological problem of the doomsday prophecy mentality lies just here—it overlooks the fact that the age to come or the last days dawned with the first coming of Christ (Acts 2:16-17; Heb 1:2; 1 Tim 4:1; 2 Tim 3:1; 1 Jn 2:18). The net result of this reality was that the early church apparently relativized time and current events. This perspective delivered the church from a crisis in confidence when the parousia (the Second Coming of Christ) did not occur in the first generation A.D. C. E. B. Cranfield expresses the point well:

> It is well known that very many scholars regard it as an assured result that the primitive Church was convinced that the End would certainly occur within, at the most, a few decades, and that its conviction has been refuted by the indisputable fact of nineteen hundred years of subsequent history. The true explanation, we

believe, is rather that the primitive Church was convinced that the ministry of Jesus had ushered in the last days, the End-time. History's supreme events had taken place in the ministry, death, resurrection and ascension of the Messiah. There was now no question of another chapter's being added which could in any way effectively go back upon what had been written in that final chapter. All that subsequent history could add, whether it should last for few years or for many, must be of the nature of an epilogue.[26]

This is a perspective conspicuously absent in modern doomsday preaching. Rather than focusing on the significance of Jesus' life, death and resurrection, such well-intentioned people are preoccupied with current events in the hopes that therein lies the only fulfillment of biblical prophecy. Ironically, however, their sincere hopes time and time again become failed prophecies that actually contribute to a sort of contemporary "delay of the parousia" complex.

Reading Current Events Back into Biblical Prophecy

We said before that in trying to make prophecy relevant, modern doomsayers are not unlike the Qumran interpreters (c. 150 B.C. to A.D. 70), who practiced a hermeneutical technique called *pesher* (Aramaic for "interpretation"). The Qumranites believed that the prophetic Scriptures, veiled to the contemporaries of the Old Testament prophets, were being properly interpreted and fulfilled only now by their own community, the true people of God. The procedure was to quote a biblical text and then state how the prophecy was fulfilled by the Qumran community. This is nicely illustrated in their commentary on Habakkuk, from which we supply the following examples (1:116— 2:15). Note the occurrences of the word *pesher* in parentheses:

Habakkuk 1:5:	1:116	Look among the nations and see, and you will be astounded, bewildered. For I will do a work in your days; you will not believe when
	2:1	it is told.
Interpretation:		The explanation of this concerns *(pesher)* those who have betrayed with the Man
	2:2	of Lies; for they have not believed the words of the Teacher of Righteousness which he received from the mouth

	2:3	of God. And it concerns those who betrayed the New Covenant, for they did not
	2:4	believe in the Covenant of God and profaned His Holy Name
Interpretation:	2:5	And likewise, the explanation of this word concerns (*pesher*) those who will betray at the end
	2:6	of day: they are the violent . . . who will not believe
	2:7	when they hear all the things which will befall the last generation from the mouth
	2:8	of the Priest whom God placed in the House of Judah to explain all
	2:9	the words of His servants the Prophets, by whose hand God has told
	2:10	all that will befall His people and the nations.
Habakkuk 1:6a		For behold, I rouse
	2:11	the Chaldeans, that cruel and hasty nation.
Interpretation:	2:12	The explanation of this concerns (*pesher*) the Kittim who are quick and valiant
	2:13	in battle, causing many to perish; and the earth will fall under the dominion
	2:14	of the Kittim. And the wicked will see it but will believe
	2:15	in the prophets of God.

What the commentary does here is to apply the prophecies of Habakkuk regarding the invasion of Judah by the Babylonian army in 587 B.C. exclusively to its own day and the invasion of Palestine by the Romans (Kittim) in 63 B.C.

It is not difficult to see that modern-day doomsday prophets unknowingly employ *pesher*-like hermeneutics when they argue that biblical prophecy is being fulfilled in their very day. A sample of typical statements by rather recent predictive preachers is easily obtained: Harold Camping claims that the last generation began with the reestablishment of Israel in 1948, in fulfillment of Mark 13:28-30.[27] In his book *Armageddon*, Grant R. Jeffrey declares that the year 2000 "is a probable termination date for the last days."[28] Chuck Smith, famous West Coast pastor, writes in his book *Future Survival* (published in 1978) that he was "convinced that the Lord is coming for His church before the end of 1981."[29] In 1977 Salem Kirban equates the Africanized "killer honeybee" with the fifth trumpet judgment of the Tribulation period described in Revelation 9:2-12.[30] Pat Robertson, one-time presidential candidate and founder of Christian Broadcasting Network, once guaranteed that the Tribulation would occur in

1982 and would be sparked by a Russian invasion of Israel (undoubtedly in fulfillment of Ezek 38—39).[31] At the end of 1992, televangelist Jack Van Impe made this appeal to his viewing audience:

Beloved, it is vital that you and I understand endtimes Bible prophecy! We *must* know what the Bible says about the Antichrist, the revived Roman Empire, the Rapture of the church, the return of Christ, Armageddon, and His Millennial Kingdom. . . . Because such signs are happening with great rapidity before our very eyes, I believe the President of the U.S.A. during the next eight years may face horrendous decisions concerning World War III and even Armageddon.

Many more doomsday *pesher*-like interpreters could be added to this list, including Charles Taylor,[32] James McKeever,[33] Mary Stewart Relfe[34] and Wim Malgo.[35] In the midst of these prophecy-prognosticators, however, at least one preacher has issued a warning about the potential harm that results from date-setting. David A. Lewis is a Springfield, Missouri, prophecy teacher who zealously monitors all date-setting schemes in his *Prophecy Intelligence Digest.* Lewis thinks every end-times Bible buff ought to sign his 1988 "Manifesto on Date Setting":

Whereas the Scripture clearly says that no man can know the day or hour of the Lord's coming, thus indicating that date-setting serves no good purpose,

And whereas date-setting has historically always proven to be false prophecy which is damaging to the cause of Christ,

And whereas we are living in the last days and nothing must be allowed to detract from the nobility and power of the message of endtime Bible prophecy,

Therefore we, the undersigned hereby demand that all date-setting and date-suggesting cease immediately. Let abstinence from this type of speculation prevail until the Lord comes.

We absolutely must stop this type of activity or there will be few who will take the message of prophecy seriously—not unlike what happened to the shepherd boy who cried wolf!

2

The Signs of the Times
Doomsday Prophecy & Theological Balance

T HE FIRST CHAPTER COULD PERHAPS HAVE GIVEN THE IMPRES-
sion that we do not believe in the imminent return of Christ, but that
is not the case. We do believe Christ could come any moment.
However, we are not bound to a particular time frame that warrants
the conclusion that Christ must return in our generation, because we
understand the fundamental end-time perspective of the New Testament to be the overlapping of the two ages. That is, the age to come
was inaugurated in this present age, with the first coming of Jesus
Christ. The upshot of this view is that Christ could come today or he
might not come for a thousand years. The ethical ramifications of this
approach are far-reaching, as one observer notes:

> Any theology that does not live with a sense of the immediate
> return of Christ is a theology that takes the edge off the urgency
> of faith. But any theology that does not cause us to live as though
> the world will be here for thousands of years is a theology that

leads us into social irresponsibility.[1]

We can probe the point more deeply. Classical dispensationalism, the tradition out of which many doomsayers seem to come, has, in our opinion, mistakenly assumed the "postponed kingdom" theory. This theory states that, with the Jews' rejection of Jesus, the kingdom of God was placed on hold, awaiting the arrival of the last days for its appearance on earth.[2] The unfortunate result of this erroneous perception is that classical dispensationalists, using *pesher* hermeneutics, go on to argue that the last days only recently began, with the reconstitution of Israel as a nation in 1948. In other words, we are now living in the last generation (see Mk 13:30, according to their interpretation). Sadly, however, reading the New Testament this way has led many classical dispensationalists to absolutize this present generation and, inevitably, has locked them into the year A.D. 2000 for the date of Christ's return.

Progressive dispensationalists, however, along with theologians of other traditions, see things differently. These scholars, rightly we believe, understand the New Testament as proclaiming the arrival of the last days with Jesus and his generation.[3] That is to say, the kingdom of God and the signs of the times began with the first coming of Christ and will continue until the parousia. As a result of this view, no particular generation, the current one included, is absolutized. Rather, time is relativized; Jesus may or may not return today. This viewpoint properly taps into the eschatological tension that characterizes the time between the first and second comings of Christ. The merit of this approach is that it is faithful to the New Testament's theme of the imminency of Christ's return but does not restrict it to a particular time frame. This perspective delivers one from a doomsday, date-setting mentality. The present chapter will fill out the details of this approach by demonstrating that the signs of the times began with Jesus and his generation. But before tackling that task, we first provide a summary statement of the biblical concept of the day of the Lord and its related concept, the last days.

The day of the Lord[4] is a standard feature in Jewish eschatological expectations. In the Old Testament, the day of the Lord designated, among other things, the final visitation of God to establish his kingdom, delivering the righteous and judging the wicked (Joel 3:1; Zeph 1:14). In the New Testament, as well as in early Judaism, the term is an expression for the arrival of the age to come that will terminate this present age. It will not be a single day but a period of the climactic outworking of the divine plan (Acts 2:20; 1 Thess 5:2; 2 Thess 2:2; 2 Pet 3:10). Alongside the day of the Lord, particularly in Paul's writings, is the term *day of Christ,* which refers to the same basic concept and elevates Jesus to the status of Yahweh (1 Cor 1:8; Phil 1:6, 10; 2:16; 2 Thess 1:10; 2 Tim 1:8), signifying that in his ministry that day has already dawned. Related terms to the day of the Lord/Christ in the New Testament are the "last days" (Acts 2:17; 2 Tim 3:1; Heb 1:2; Jas 5:3; 2 Pet 3:3; compare 1 Tim 4:1) and "the last hour" (1 Jn 2:18), both of which make clear that the end time has broken into this present age, beginning with the death and resurrection of Christ. All of the foregoing terms witness to the belief in early Christianity that the age to come had already begun, though it was not yet complete.

The Signs of the Times

The bulk of this chapter will be devoted to defending the thesis that the signs of the times began with Jesus and his generation. The Old Testament and Judaism associated the appearance of the age to come on earth with a number of events: the rise of the antichrist; the messianic woes (wars, earthquakes, famines, persecution of the righteous, apostasy from the faith, cosmic disturbances); the arrival of the kingdom of God; judgment of the wicked and the resurrection of the righteous; and the new creation. These events were subsumed under the category of the day of the Lord or the last days. We do not wish to give the impression that all of these attendant circumstances were treated with equal interest in the pertinent Jewish writings; in actuality some were of more concern to certain authors than others. But, in general, these events were equated with the signs of the times; hence their occurrence in a number of Jewish works. The basic point to be made in what follows is that, for the New Testament, these happenings fall under the rubric of the already/not yet eschatological tension.

More specifically, in large part, we will utilize the framework of the signs of the times as outlined in Jesus' Olivet Discourse (especially Mt 24; Mk 13; Lk 21; compare Rev 6). We will attempt to confirm what numerous scholars have argued—the signs of the times began with Jesus and his generation, especially with Jesus' death and resurrection, together with the fall of Jerusalem in A.D. 70. The latter event serves as the backdrop for Jesus' description of the parousia. In effect, according to the Olivet Discourse, the fall of Jerusalem is a part of the "already" aspect of the age to come, while the return of Christ constitutes its "not yet" aspect. We now proceed to delineate the signs of the times according to that schematic: the rise of the antichrist; the messianic woes; the arrival of the kingdom of God; judgment of the wicked and the resurrection of the righteous; and the new creation.

The Rise of the Antichrist

It is a commonplace among Gospel scholars today to view the Olivet Discourse of Jesus (Mt 24; Mk 13; Lk 21) as portraying the parousia against the backdrop of the fall of Jerusalem. For example, in his magisterial commentary on Luke, Joseph A. Fitzmyer writes of Luke 21:

> The Lucan discourse looks back at the catastrophe on Jerusalem (A.D. 70) in a microcosmic view; it sees the crisis that the earthly coming of Jesus brought into the lives of his own generation, but sees it now as a harbinger of the crisis which Jesus and his message, and above all his coming as the Son of Man, will bring to "all who dwell upon the entire face of the earth" (21:35). Both of the events are examples for Luke of God's judgment. . . . As Jerusalem met its fate, so will all who dwell upon the face of the earth.[5]

Two of the key phrases in the Olivet Discourse highlighting the connection between the fall of Jerusalem and the parousia are "the beginning of birth pangs" and the "end is not yet" (Mt 24:6-8; Mk 13:7-8; compare Lk 21:9). These phrases convey the idea that the signs of the times *began* with Jesus and his generation, especially the fall of Jerusalem, but will not be complete until the return of Christ.

This pattern, as a number of scholars have argued, also seems to fit the book of Revelation.[6] Recognizing this enables one to associate the signs of the times describing the fall of Jerusalem in the Olivet Discourse with the judgments delineated in the Apocalypse, especially the seal judgments of Revelation 6, the prototype of the trumpet and bowl judgments. R. H. Charles notes the following connections:

Matthew 24:6-7, 9a, 29
1. Wars
2. International strife
3. Famines
4. Earthquakes
5. Persecutions
6. Eclipses of the sun and moon; falling of the stars; shaking of the power of heaven

Mark 13:7-9a, 24-25
1. Wars
2. International strife
3. Earthquakes
4. Famines
5. Persecutions
6. (As in Matthew)

Luke 21:9-12a, 25-26
1. Wars
2. International strife
3. Earthquakes
4. Famines

5. Pestilence
6. Persecutions

Revelation 6:2-17; 7:1
Seal 1. Wars
Seal 2. International strife
Seal 3. Famine
Seal 4. Pestilence (Death and Hades)
Seal 5. Persecutions
Seal 6. (6:12-7:3) Earthquakes, eclipse of the sun, ensanguining of the moon . . .[7]

The conclusion to be drawn from these comparisons is that the three Gospels and the Apocalypse view the signs of the times as having already begun in Jesus' generation, particularly with the fall of Jerusalem. The task that lies before us, therefore, is to root the preceding signs of the times in, and around, the events surrounding the fall of Jerusalem.

Although Charles's chart does not spell out the first sign of the time, the rise of antichrist, such a personage is clearly alluded to in the Olivet Discourse, and also probably in Revelation 6:2 and elsewhere in the New Testament. Judaism associated the end times with the figure of the antichrist, who would arrive on the world scene to do battle with God and his people.[8] Though the name is the product of Christian thought, the idea of an end-time, anti-God personage has its roots in the Old Testament, especially in Ezekiel 38—39. There, Gog of the land of Magog is identified as the leader of the forces of evil in opposition to God. Hermann Gunkel traces the concept even further back to the primeval past, to the supposed conflict between God and the primeval monster Chaos, a creature given various names: dragon (Job 7:12; Ps 74:13; Is 51:9; Ezek 2:3; 32:2); Leviathan (Job 40:15-24; Pss 74:14; 104:26; Is 27:1); Rahab (Job 9:13; 26:12; Ps 89:10; Is 30:7; 51:9); serpent (Job 26:13; Is 27:1; Amos 9:3); Tehom/Tiamat (Gen 1:2, 6; Ps 74:13); and others.[9] These notions of an end-time anti-God personage and a primeval chaotic beast combined to produce the multivalent figure of the antichrist. H. H. Rowley describes him thus:

Whether regarded as a mere man or as the incarnation of this demonic spirit, we have the figure of a powerful king or ruler, subduing many beneath his evil sway, filled with the sense of his own importance, setting himself up to be equal with God, claiming divine honours, and trampling on the saints.[10]

References to this malevolent force abound: Daniel 7:8, 25; 11:36, 40-41, 45; *Assumption of Moses* 8:1; *Psalms of Solomon* 2:29; *1 Ezra* 5:6; *Testament of Isaac* 6:1; *Testament of Judah* 25:3; *Testament of Dan* 5:4; *Sibylline Oracles* 2:63, 75; 2 Thessalonians 2:3-12; 1 John 4:3; Revelation 11:7, 13; 13:2, 5, 7.

A number of these passages call for comment, especially the New Testament references. Second Thessalonians 2:3-12 is the key Pauline text on the antichrist, who is portrayed there as the man of lawlessness. According to Paul, although the person of the antichrist has not yet appeared on the human scene (2 Thess 2:3-6, 8-12), the *spirit* of antichrist, the "mystery of lawlessness," is already at work (v. 7). The only force preventing the antichrist from making his grand entry is the restrainer.[11] A similar idea is conveyed by 1 John 4:3: "But every spirit that does not acknowledge Jesus is not from God. This is the spirit of the antichrist, which you have heard is coming and even now is already in the world."

It is this same thought that informs the Olivet Discourse and its reference to the false Christs, as depicted in Matthew (24:4-5, 11-12, 23-26); Mark (13:5-6, 21-23); and Luke (21:8). Messianic claimants abounded in Palestine in the first century (see Acts 5:36-37; 21:38; Josephus, *Antiquities of the Jews* 18.4.1; 20.5.1; 20.8.6). Jesus' usage of apocalyptic language to describe the activity of such pseudo-messiahs is similar to the warnings of the first-century Jewish historian Josephus who, for example, provides a commentary on the tragic results for those who were deceived by the false predictions of self-styled prophets at the fall of Jerusalem. As we saw in chapter one, Josephus tells of six thousand Jews who perished in the flames of the temple porticoes at the time of the Roman destruction of the temple in A.D. 70. They had been deluded by a false prophet, who had on that day announced to the people in the city that God commanded them to go to the temple to receive the signs of their salvation (*Jewish Wars* 6.5.2-3).

The idea that the spirit of the antichrist appeared during Jesus' generation seems to extend to the Apocalypse, especially Revelation 6:2; 13:1-18; 17:8-13. Though these enigmatic texts will probably never be fully grasped this side of heaven, situating them approximately in the time of Emperor Nero (A.D. 54-68) will help clarify the picture. Drawing on the research of others, we will briefly analyze each text in light of his era.

Probably the best understanding of the first horseman of the Apocalypse (Rev 6:2) is that it refers to the antichrist.[12] The symbolism of the white horse, bow and crown serves as a parody of Christ (Rev 19:11-19). A popular interpretation of this seal judgment is that it describes the ancient Parthians, using apocalyptic language. The Parthians were expert horsemen and archers, and they posed a constant threat to the Roman Empire in the first century. They were always poised to cross the Euphrates River, and in A.D. 62 their military leader, Vologesus, did attack some Roman legions. The Parthians rode white horses and their founder, Seleucus, was named Nikator, "the victor."[13] These descriptions help to give the background of Revelation 6:2.

Furthermore if, as a number of scholars feel, the beast of Revelation 13:3 (compare Rev 17:11), who received a mortal wound in the head but was revived, draws on the Nero Redivivus (Revived) story, then the Parthian background of Revelation 6:2 is strengthened in the following way. Although Nero's first five years as emperor were relatively good, it was all downhill after that. He perpetrated one monstrosity after the next, including the murders of foes, friends and family, sodomy, tyranny and persecution of Christians (A.D. 64).[14] Indeed, the title "beast" was a fitting one for him (Rev 13:1). So unpopular was Nero that toward the end of his reign, in A.D. 67-68, there were open revolts against his authority in Gaul and Spain. Eventually, the Praetorian Guard and the Senate proclaimed him to be a public enemy and approved Galba as his successor. Nero fled and reportedly committed suicide by thrusting a sword through his throat on June 9, A.D. 68. However, the rumor spread that he had not died but escaped to Parthia and would return with the Parthian army to regain his throne. Hence the story of Nero Redivivus. This fearful expectation of the return of Nero, a type of the antichrist, leading the Parthian cavalry riding on white horses with bows and arrows, going forth to conquer, makes good sense of the first horseman of the Apocalypse. *Sibylline Oracles* 4:119-127, a first-century Jewish writing, provides a combined description of the Nero Redivivus story and the destruction of Jerusalem by the Roman general, Titus, in A.D. 70:

> And then from Italy a great king, like a fugitive slave, shall flee unseen, unheard of, over the passage of the Euphrates; when he shall dare even the hateful pollution of a mother's murder, and many other things beside, venturing so far with wicked hand. And many for the throne of Rome shall dye the ground with their blood, when he has run away beyond the Parthian land. And a Roman leader [Titus] shall come to Syria, who shall burn down Solyma's [sic] temple with fire, and therewith slay many men, and shall waste the great land of the Jews with its broad way.

This background also sheds light on Revelation 13:1-18. Examining this text through the Neronian backdrop provides a clearer perspective on these otherwise baffling verses. Nero's infamous character merits the title of "beast" applied to him by the seer of the Apocalypse (v. 1). Revelation 13:1-6 gives the generic background of the beast, which is the Roman Empire of the first century. The seven heads correspond to the seven hills of Rome, while the ten horns allude to the Caesars of the first century, however one may number them (v. 1).[15] The blasphemous worship demanded by the beast distinctly reminds one of the imperial cult of the first century, and the war the beast wages on the saints cannot help but recall the intense persecutions Nero, and later Domitian, inflicted on Christians because they did not worship Caesar.

Besides this generic background, there may also be specific allusions in this text to Nero himself, the precursor of the antichrist. We have already noted his beastly character (v. 1) and his alleged recovery (v. 3). Nero's persecution of Christians from November A.D. 64 to June A.D. 68 could account, in part, for the forty-two months (or three and one-half years) of oppression mentioned in Revelation 13:5. The reference in Revelation 13:10 to those who kill with the sword being killed by the sword reminds one simultaneously of Nero's persecution of Christians and his own apparent suicide by the sword. The reference in Revelation 13:11-15 to the beast of the land securing worship for the beast from the sea (Rome was across the sea from the place of the writing of the Apocalypse, Asia Minor) reminds one of the local priests of the imperial cult in Asia Minor whose task was to compel the people to offer a sacrifice to Caesar and proclaim him Lord. Megalomaniac that he was, Nero had coins minted in which he was called "almighty God" and "Savior." Nero's portrait also appears on coins as the god Apollo playing a lyre. While earlier emperors were proclaimed deities upon their deaths, Nero abandoned all reserve and demanded divine honors while still alive (as did also Caligula before him, A.D. 37-41). Those who worshiped the emperor received a certificate or mark of approval—*charagma,* the same word used in Revelation 13:16. Furthermore, in the reign of Emperor Decius (A.D. 249-251), those who did not possess the certificate of sacrifice to Caesar could not pursue trades, a prohibition that conceivably goes back to Nero, reminding one of Revelation 13:17. Finally, in the number 666 (Rev 13:18) one can detect the apocalyptic seer's usage of gematria, a mathematic cryptogram which assigns numerical values to letters of the alphabet. More than one scholar has seen a possible referent of this number in *Neron Kaiser.* The Hebrew numerical valuation for *Nrwn Qsr* is as follows: N = 50, R = 200, W = 6, N = 50, Q = 100, S = 60 and R = 200, which add up to 666.[16]

The Neronian background also throws light on Revelation 17:8-13. The same metaphors rooted in the Roman Empire occur here—seven heads/hills and ten horns/Caesars with blasphemous names demanding worship. The added detail concerns the identification of the beast who "was and is not, and is about to come out of the abyss" (v. 8). More specific information about this personage is supplied in verses 10-11. According to Charles, the fifth king "who was and is to come" is Nero (in particular, the story of Nero Redivivus): Augustus (31 B.C.-A.D. 14), Tiberius (A.D. 14-37), Caligula (A.D. 37-41), Claudius (A.D. 41-54), Nero (A.D. 54-68). Moreover, notes Charles, the king "who is," is Vespasian (A.D. 69-79, discounting the short and ineffective reigns of Galba [A.D. 68-69], Otho [A.D. 69] and Vitellius [A.D. 69]). The "other who has not yet come, and when he comes, must remain a little while" is, according to Charles, Titus (A.D. 79-81), who died after a short reign.[17]

Utilizing this historical framework also helps to uncover the meaning of Revelation 17:1-7. The apostle John describes there a harlot, full of blasphemous names, sitting on the beast. A number of commentators, rightly in our estimation, identify the harlot with unfaithful Israel, especially Jerusalem.[18] The description in verse 6 of the harlot's killing of the martyrs is distinctly reminiscent of Jesus' accusations against Jerusalem (Mt 23:29-39). The city's idolatry also recalls Israel's past unfaithfulness to God, in this instance manifested in first-century Judaism's privileged religious status before Rome.[19] Early Jewish Christians, however, did not share this status, as they were expelled from the synagogues, thereby being forced to face Caesar worship.[20] When John speaks of the beast turning on the harlot and destroying her (vv. 16-18), he in all probability alludes to the divine judgment that befell Jerusalem for cooperating with the imperial cult. The destruction of Jerusalem in A.D. 70 also seems to be drawn upon in Revelation 11:2, where it is said that the outer court of the temple "has been given to the Gentiles. They will trample on the holy city" (compare Lk 21:24).

Our treatment of Revelation 6:2, 13:1-18 and 17:8-13 does not imply that Nero filled the complete expectation of the coming antichrist, but, as a precursor to such, he is certainly a good starting place. Adding to this equation the other New Testament texts assembled—Mark 13:5-6 (compare the other Synoptic references); 2 Thessalonians 2; 1 John 4:3—permits one to say that the sign of the rise of the spirit of antichrist began in Jesus' generation, particularly with a ruler like Nero and with an event like the fall of Jerusalem. It is against such a backdrop that the return of Christ is painted in the Olivet Discourse. Thus, the signs of the times were initiated long ago, not in 1948 with the regathering of Israel to its rightful land. And it remains a matter of speculation when these signs will be completed, precipitating the return of Christ.

The Messianic Woes
In Judaism the messianic woes refer to the time of great sorrow and tribulation to come upon God's people immediately prior to the coming of the Messiah. The concept is foreshadowed in the Old Testament, in association with the day of Yahweh (see, for example, Is 24:17-23; Dan 12:1; Joel 2:1-11, 28-32; Amos 5:16-20; Zeph 1:14—2:3) and developed in Jewish apocalypticism (4 Ezra 7:37; *Jubilees* 23:11; 24:3; *2 Apocalypse of Baruch* 55:6; *1 Enoch* 80:4-5). The term itself, however, does not occur until the writing of the Talmud (for example, *b. Šabbat* 118a; *b. Pesaḥim* 118a). A number of events were often associated with the messianic woes: wars, earthquakes, famines, the persecution of God's people, the apostasy of God's people and cosmic disturbances. The point we wish to make in this section is that the messianic woes began with Jesus and his generation, and we will continue to base our comments primarily on the Olivet Discourse.

1. Wars (Mt 24:6-7; Mk 13:7-8; Lk 21:9-10; compare Rev 6:3-4). Often doomsday preachers assert that this current generation is witnessing a proliferation of wars and that, therefore, we are in the last generation. While we do not wish to minimize the horrors of modern-day warfare, it is important to note that strife and conflict have always been a part of the human experience. In Mark 13:7-8, Jesus himself acknowledged the certainty of war but added that war was not necessarily the sign of the end. It, like other signs of the times, was only the beginning of "birth pangs" or the messianic woes.

It is quite probable that, rather than referring to our generation, the wars and rumors of wars Jesus referred to occurred, at least in part, in his generation, especially at the time of the destruction of Jerusalem. Many scholars believe that Jesus' reference to the increase in wars as reflected in the Gospels and Revelation 6:3-4 (the second horseman) alludes to the first century. The peace that Caesar Augustus (31 B.C.-A.D. 14) established *(pax Romana)* throughout the Roman Empire was short-lived. Wars broke out in Britain, Germany, Armenia and Parthia under Emperor Claudius between A.D. 41 and 54. The period following Nero's death (A.D. 69) saw three emperors, Otho, Galba and Vitellius, quickly rise and fall, amidst civil upheavals and political chaos. So devastating was the period following Nero's death that it threatened to reduce the Roman Empire to rubble. The peril Rome faced at that time was well known by that generation. Josephus could write of the Roman civil wars, "I have omitted to give an exact account of them, because they are well known by all, and they are described by a great number of Greek and Roman authors" *(Jewish Wars* 4.9.2; compare Tacitus *Histories* 1.2-3 and Seutonius *Lives,* "Vespasian" 1). Some modern-day commentators go so far as to see the restoration of the beast referred to in Revelation 13:3 and 17:11 as depicting the survival and revival of the Roman Empire out of such chaos.[21]

Especially relevant to the end-time sign of wars and rumors of wars was the Jewish revolt against Rome, which culminated in the fall of Jerusalem (A.D. 66-70). The Jewish war against Rome witnessed the deaths of thousands and thousands of Jews in Judea and the enslavement of thousands more. Josephus estimates that as many as 1,100,000 Jews were killed at that time (though he undoubtedly exaggerated the figure). Titus, the Roman general, razed the city to the ground. Josephus writes of this:

> Now, as soon as the army had no more people to slay or to plunder, because there remained none to be objects of their fury (for they would not have spared any, had there remained any other such work to be done) Caesar gave orders that they should now demolish the entire city and temple, but should leave as many of the towers

standing as were of the greatest eminency; that is, Phasaelus, and Hippicus, and Mariamne, and so much of the wall as enclosed the city on the west side. This wall was spared, in order to afford a camp for such as were to lie in garrison; as were the towers also spared, in order to demonstrate to posterity what kind of city it was, and how well fortified, which the Roman valor had subdued; but for all the rest of the wall, it was so thoroughly laid even with the ground by those that dug it up to the foundation, that there was left nothing to make those that came thither believe it had ever been inhabited. This was the end which Jerusalem came to by the madness of those that were for innovations; a city otherwise of great magnificence, and of mighty fame among all mankind. (*Jewish Wars* 7.1.1)

For Josephus, the destruction of Jerusalem was beyond comparison. He observes:

Whereas the war which the Jews made with the Romans has been the greatest of all those, not only that have been in our times, but, in a manner, of those that ever were heard of; both of those wherein cities have fought against cities, or nations against nations. ... Accordingly it appears to me, that the misfortunes of all men, from the beginning of the world, if they be compared to these of the Jews, are not so considerable as they were. (*Jewish Wars,* preface to 1 and 4)

Jesus' prophecy about the city had come true (Mt 24:15; Mk 13:14; Lk 19:41-44; 21:20-24; Rev 6:3-4; 11:1-2 [compare v. 8]; 17—18).

2. Earthquakes (Mt 24:7; Mk 13:8; Lk 21:11; Rev 11:13; compare Mt 27:51-53; 28:2-4). Repeatedly one hears doomsday prophets say that earthquakes are on the increase, indicating that we are living in the last generation. Aside from the lack of documentation supporting the theory of increased earthquakes,[22] there is a better time frame through which to interpret Jesus' reference to earthquakes—namely, such portents signified that the last days began in his generation. Actually, the verses describing the eventuality of earthquakes point to two historic fulfillments—the fall of Jerusalem in A.D. 70 (Mt 24:7; Mk 13:8; Lk 21:11; Rev 11:13) and the cross and resurrection of Jesus in A.D. 33 (Mt 27:51-53; 28:2-4).

The context of Jesus' prediction about earthquakes is the fall of

Jerusalem (compare Mt 24:7 with v. 15; Mk 13:8 with v. 14; Lk 21:11 with vv. 20-24), as it is for John's utterance (compare Rev 11:13 with vv. 1-8).[23] Although we have no historical record of an earthquake occurring at the time of the fall of Jerusalem, the figure given in Revelation 11:13 is not without historical verisimilitude. That passage speaks of an earthquake during which a tenth of the city fell, killing seven thousand people, an amount commensurate with the population of Jerusalem in Jesus' generation (approximately seventy thousand).[24]

But the fall of Jerusalem may not exhaust the time frame predicated for Jesus' prophecy about earthquakes. His own death and resurrection may also factor into the equation. In a fascinating analysis of Matthew 27:51-53, Dale C. Allison convincingly argues that the earthquakes and the resurrection of the saints described there that accompanied Jesus' death and resurrection were a signal that the signs of the times were initiated with the passion of Christ. In particular, Allison demonstrates that Matthew 27:51-53 should be understood as a partial fulfillment of Zechariah 14:4-7, a text predicting the descent of the Messiah to the Mount of Olives, resulting in an earthquake and the resurrection of the righteous.[25] Allison extends his thesis to include Matthew 28:2-4, where the twofold event of earthquake and resurrection characterizes Jesus as well.[26] Allison agrees with the conclusion of Eduard Schweizer regarding this passage: "All the elements [of Mt 28:2-4] recall the signs expected to accompany the coming of the Lord at the end of the world and the irruption of the kingdom of God."[27]

These two incidents, the apparent earthquake during the fall of Jerusalem and the one accompanying the passion of Jesus, conveyed two very different messages. The former forecast destruction while the latter signified deliverance. However, both were eschatological in import—the signs of the times had already begun.

3. Famines (Mt 24:7; Mk 13:8; Lk 21:11; Rev 6:5-6). The inevitable consequence of war is famine, nowhere so starkly depicted as in Revelation 6:5-6, with its description of the third horseman. It would have been easy for the seer of the Apocalypse to envision war and famine. During Claudius's reign, famine occurred in Rome in A.D. 42 and food shortage was reported in Judea in 45-46, in Greece in 49 and in Rome again in 51. The reference to the pair of scales and the inflated prices for food in Revelation 6:5-6 cannot help but recall the severe famine that occurred in Jerusalem during its siege by the Roman army. During that time the inhabitants of Jerusalem had to weigh out their food and drink because of the scarcity of those necessities. So severe was the famine that even the love of a mother for her child ceased. Josephus records the story about Mary, a woman from Perea, who was among the Jews starving in Jerusalem during its siege. She seized her child, an infant at her breast, slew it and roasted it for food for herself (*Jewish Wars* 6.3.4; compare 6.5.1; compare Lk 21:23). Again, Josephus gives emphatic testimony to the role of famine during the Jewish war against Rome:

> But the famine was too hard for all other passions, and it is destructive to nothing so much as to modesty; for what was otherwise worthy of reverence, was in this case despised; insomuch that children pulled the very morsels that their fathers were eating, out of their very mouths, and what was still more to be pitied, so did the mothers do as to their infants. (*Jewish Wars* 5.10.5)

The fall of Jerusalem and the resulting famine may also explain the ironic statement in Revelation 6:6, "and do not harm the oil and the wine." The command to spare the oil and the wine quite possibly is an allusion to General Titus's order that even during the ransacking of Jerusalem, olive trees (for oil) and grape vines (for wine) were to be spared.[28] If so, the fall of Jerusalem serves as the perfect backdrop for the third seal judgment (Rev 6:5-6), as it does for the Olivet Discourse prophecy about the eventuality of famines. Indeed, Jesus' statement that such horrors were but the beginning of the end (Mk 13:7), the initiation of the messianic woes (Mk 13:8), points in that direction (compare Rev 6:7-8 and the fourth seal judgment).[29]

4. Persecution (Mt 24:9-10; Mk 13:9-19; Lk 21:12-19; Rev 6:9-11). There are three interlocking destinies delineated in the Olivet Discourse and the fifth seal judgment of Revelation: the persecution of Jesus' disciples, Jesus' crucifixion and the destruction of Jerusalem. The apparent connection to be made from this is that Israel's crucifixion of Jesus and subsequent persecution of his disciples brought about divine destruction on Jerusalem.

The Olivet Discourse ominously predicts that Jesus' disciples will be persecuted (Mt 24:9-10; Mk 13:9-19; Lk 21:12-19). Luke's second volume, Acts, records the fulfillment of Jesus' prediction, describing the persecutions of Peter and John (Acts 4:1-12; compare 12:3-19), Stephen (Acts 6:8—7:60), James (Acts 12:1-2), Paul (Acts 16:22-30; 21:28—23:35) and many other Jewish Christians (Acts 8:1-4). In being delivered up to the Jewish and Roman authorities, the disciples were repeating the destiny of Jesus (see the threefold passion predictions—Mk 8:31; 9:31; 10:33-34—and obviously the crucifixion account itself). Allison has carefully demonstrated that such affliction was understood by early Christians as the beginning of the messianic woes, a time of unparalleled persecution of God's people that was expected to immediately precede the arrival of the kingdom of God.[30]

Later church tradition understood that the fall of Jerusalem in A.D. 70 came about as a result of divine judgment because of the Jewish persecution of Jesus' followers. For example, Eusebius, the fourth-century church historian, refers to the belief of many that God judged Jerusalem because it killed the half-brother of Jesus, James the Just (*Ecclesiastical History* 2.23). Even Josephus attributed Jerusalem's fall to divine judgment. Writing of the burning and destruction of the temple in late August/early September A.D. 70, he writes that the fire was not ultimately ignited by the Romans: "The flames . . . owed their origin and cause to God's own people" (*Jewish Wars* 6.4.5).

The same threefold intertwined destinies emerge from Revelation 6:9-11, the fifth seal judgment. That the martyrs described therein are Christians is rather plain. A corresponding description of these tribulation saints occurs in Revelation 7:9-17 and 14:1-5. Their exemplar in suffering for righteousness is Jesus, the Lamb that was slain (Rev 5:6-14). But who were the perpetrators of such injustice and violence upon the people of God? Revelation 6:10 provides a clue—it was "the inhabitants of the earth" (compare 3:10; 11:10). While the phrase can mean "the inhabitants of the world," the more likely meaning of the phrase in Revelation 6:10 is "the inhabitants of the land [Palestine]." Alan James Beagley describes these "earth-dwellers" as they are portrayed in the Apocalypse:

> Rev 6:10 makes it clear that they have been involved in the persecution and slaughter of those who have preached the word of God and who have remained faithful in their witness, and it is against these persecutors in particular that the martyrs cry out to God for vengeance. Then again, it is the "earth-dwellers" who are named specifically as the victims of the three "woes" which are associated with the fifth, sixth and seventh trumpets (8:13). The same term is also used of those who have in some way suffered through the ministry of the "two witnesses" and who rejoice and exchange gifts at the death of the witnesses (Rev 11:10). It is this same group of people also who give allegiance to the beast from the sea, and they are further characterized as those whose names were "not written before the foundation of the world in the book of life of the lamb that was slain" (13:18). Finally, in chapter 17 the "earth-dwellers" are associated with the harlot, "Babylon," and with the scarlet beast on which she rides: they have become drunk with the wine of the harlot's fornication (v 2) and they are overawed at the beast and its apparent permanence (v 8).[31]

Beagley's interpretation is that the inhabitants of Jerusalem are being described.[32] Others concur. Philip Carrington, for example, sees in the phrase "the earth-dwellers"

> an indication that the Seer is thinking of a judgment which is to fall on Jerusalem, since there is in the martyrs' cry the first clear echo of the words of Jesus; for he says that there shall come upon you all the Righteous Blood which is being shed upon the Land from the Blood of Righteous Abel to the Blood of Zacharias son of Barachias, whom ye murdered between the Naos and the Altar: verily, I say unto you all these shall come upon this generation (Matt. xxiii.35). Not only is the symbol of blood revenge the same; but it points out what later study will confirm; it is the land of Israel, and in particular the Temple at Jerusalem which is to suffer. And we must remember that there is a hint of the same idea in the Four Seals; for the Four Judgments in Ezekiel, to which they correspond, were all to come upon Jerusalem.[33]

5. Apostasy (Mt 24:10-13; Mk 13:20-23; Lk 21:34-36). Related to the rise of the antichrist was the concept of apostasy, a Jewish apocalyptic idea that the end of time would witness a large-scale turning away from the faith by the people of God (*Jubilees* 23:14-23; 4 Ezra 5:1-13; *1 Enoch* 91:3-10; etc.). The Olivet Discourse obviously refers to that expectation (Mt 24:10-13; Mk 13:20-23; Lk 21:34-36). Three other places in the New Testament refer to that situation, each of which assumes that the end-time sign of apostasy began in Jesus' generation: the Pauline literature, the Gospel of John and Revelation 13:15-18.

Several of Paul's letters attest to the belief that the apocalyptic expectation of apostasy had already begun: 2 Thessalonians, 1 Timothy, 2 Timothy and Galatians. A brief overview of the relevant texts follows.[34]

As mentioned in connection with the antichrist, 2 Thessalonians 2:3-12 is stamped by the already/not yet eschatological tension. This applies as well to the sign of the time called "apostasy" (v. 3). The day is coming, says the apostle, when people will believe the lie of the man of lawlessness and refuse to be saved. God himself will permit that delusion to dupe many. According to verse 7, the lawlessness has already begun. It is probable that Paul had something specific in mind with reference to the present work of lawlessness, and 1 Thessalonians 2:14-17 seems to be the key—"the Jews . . . killed the Lord Jesus . . . and also drove us out . . . in their effort to keep us from speaking to the Gentiles so that they may be saved. In this way they always heap up their sins to the limit. The wrath of God has come upon them at last." What the apostle refers to here is not ethnic resentment toward his countrymen but eschatological judgment. The Jews, the people of God of old, have, in rejecting their Messiah and his messengers like Paul, become participants in the apostasy of the last days which is already at work.

First Timothy 4:1-5 and 2 Timothy 3:1-5 bear this out. Both passages speak of the coming religious apostasy in the last days (especially 1 Tim 4:1, "some will abandon the faith" and 2 Tim 3:5, "having a form of godliness but denying its power"). But that that event is already in progress is evident in the way Paul perceives his opponents as having succumbed to spiritual lawlessness (see 1 Tim 1:6-7, 19-20; 2 Tim 2:18; 3:6). Galatians 1:6-10 continues in the same vein of thought. Paul signals this background with his reference to "the present evil age" (1:4). The Galatians' temptation to embrace the rival "gospel" of Paul's opponents in Galatia, the Judaizers, sounds very much like a part of the deception that was expected to take hold of the professing people of God during the messianic woes (compare 2 Thess 2:9; Mk 13:22). In fact, the word Paul used in Galatians 1:6 of the Galatians, "deserting" *(metatithēmi)* is used in the Septuagint (the Greek translation of the Old Testament, c. 250 B.C.) to refer to religious apostasy (Sirach 6:9; 2 Maccabees 7:24; compare Josephus *Antiquities of the Jews* 20.4; *Life of Flavius Josephus* 195). Also, the word "quickly" *(tacheōs)* in Galatians 1:6 approaches the status of a *technicus terminus* for the quickness with which the messianic woes will give way to the parousia (see 2 Thess 2:2; Rev 1:1; 2:16; 3:11; 22:7, 12, 20). Moreover, the anathema Paul pronounced on his opponents who were trying to deceive the Galatians (1:8-9) definitely has an eschatological ring to it, much like the divine wrath that was expected to fall on the false prophets and pseudomessiahs at the parousia (see Mk 13:24; 1 Thess 5:9; 2 Thess 2:8).

Allison calls attention to another writer who seems to have believed that end-time apostasy began in Jesus' day—the writer of the Gospel of John. John depicted Judas Iscariot as a type of the antichrist and an apostate. Allison notes that already in 6:70 the disciple who betrayed Jesus is labeled "a devil." Later, in 13:2, one reads that it is the devil that has put it into the heart of Judas to betray Jesus, and in 13:27 that, "after the morsel, Satan entered into him." In 14:30 Jesus declares that the ruler of the world now comes, and the title seemingly refers to Judas, or to Judas as the embodiment of the evil *archōn* ("ruler"). Allison also observes that, even more significantly, in 17:12 Judas is called "the son of perdition" (KJV) or "the one doomed to destruction" (NIV). This precise phrase is used in 2 Thessalonians 2:3 to describe the coming man of lawlessness and was, perhaps, a technical term.

Paul declares that the day of the Lord will not come unless "the son of perdition"—who is not Satan himself but Satan's instrument—comes first.[35] According to C. K. Barrett, "It seems probable that John saw in Judas the eschatological character who must appear before the manifestation of the glory of Christ (just as in 1 Jn. 2:18, 22; 4:3 heretical teachers are represented as Antichrist)."[36] This conclusion, if justified, supplies one more example of the transfer to the passion narrative of an eschatological prediction. Wendy E. Sproston writes, "Whereas for Paul the glorious parousia could not take place unless the Satanically inspired 'son of perdition' had first worked the ultimate evil, for the fourth evangelist, to whom the crucifixion of Christ was synonymous with his glorification, it is the figure of Judas which symbolizes the final apostasy."[37]

A third place that indicates that the apostasy of the last days began in Jesus' generation is Revelation 13:15-18, particularly in its description of the mark of the beast. Because we earlier examined this passage relative to the rise of the antichrist, we only want to touch upon one further detail in this text—the mark of the beast on the worshiper's right hand and/or forehead may well be a parody of the Jewish phylacteries in Jesus' day. Based on Deuteronomy 6:8, Jewish males adopted the custom of tying leather boxes containing portions of the Ten Commandments to their arms and heads during their times of prayer. Seen against this backdrop, the exposure of the mark of the beast can be understood as pointing a guilty finger at those Jews in the first century who belied their commitment to monotheism by cooperating with imperial Rome. This poignantly explains why the Apocalypse refers to such people as those "who say they are Jews and are not, but are a synagogue of Satan" (Rev 2:9, 24; compare 1:7; 17:3). Their rejection of Jesus and his followers on the one hand and their acceptance, or at least condoning, of Caesar worship on the other,[38] according to the seer of the Apocalypse, was nothing less than eschatological apostasy.

6. *Cosmic Disturbances (Mt 24:29; Mk 13:24-25; Lk 21:11, 25-26; Rev 6:12-17)*. The Old Testament associated cosmic disturbances with the coming of divine judgment, especially the day of the Lord (Is 34:4;

Ezek 32:7; Joel 3:3-4; Hab 2:6, 21). That Jesus should use such apocalyptic imagery to describe the fall of Jerusalem (see especially Lk 21:11) was not unusual. Josephus did the same: "Many of those that were worn away by the famine, and their mouths almost closed, when they saw the fire of the holy house, they exerted their utmost strength, and broke out into groans and outcries again. Perea did also return the echo . . . and augmented the force of the entire noise" (*Jewish Wars* 6.5.1). Elsewhere, Josephus blames the inhabitants of Jerusalem for not recognizing God's judgment on the city and not believing the clear portents that signaled the coming desolation. So it was when a star, looking like a sword, stood over the city, and a comet lasted for a year (*Jewish Wars* 6.5.3).

The sixth seal judgment of the Apocalypse (6:12-17) seems to also utilize apocalyptic language to rehearse cosmic disturbances in the first century. The opening of the sixth seal (6:12-17) introduces several spectacular physical phenomena which strike terror into people of every social rank, so that they seek to hide from God and the Lamb. Beagley believes that this too is a reference to events of the first century. There were various earthquakes at this period, three being referred to by Tacitus (*Annals* 12.43, 58; 14.27)—in A.D. 51, 53 and 60—and others during the seventh decade being mentioned by Seneca (*Naturales Quaestiones* 6.1; 7.28). The darkening of the sun is thought to be a reference to the solar eclipses which occurred between A.D. 49 and 52, or perhaps to phenomena associated with the eruption of Vesuvius in A.D. 79. Beagley also suggests that the reference to islands being moved from their places (6:14) is connected with "the sudden formation of new islands": for example, Thera and Terasia (compare Seneca *Naturales Quaestiones* 6.2, 6). Beagley also calls attention to the connection between Revelation 6:16 and Luke 23:30, both of which allude to the destruction of Jerusalem in A.D. 70.[39]

Thus it can be argued that the messianic woes (wars, famines, earthquakes, persecution, apostasy, cosmic disturbances) are perceived by a number of New Testament authors as having begun in Jesus' generation. This is the "already" aspect of eschatology. We do not mean to suggest, however, that the messianic woes were fully exhausted by incidents in the first century. Their full significance and occurrence is still forthcoming and will ultimately lead to the return of Christ. Our purpose here has been to show that the last days did not begin in 1948 but rather with the first coming of Jesus. It is therefore not wise to assert that we must now be living in the last generation before the parousia.

The Kingdom of God

The next three signs of the times—the kingdom of God, judgment of the righteous and the wicked, and the new creation—can be treated quickly. This is so because scholars long ago such as Albert Schweitzer demonstrated that these end-time events were viewed as beginning with Jesus. We begin first with the kingdom of God, particularly in the way it was proclaimed by Jesus and Paul.

Many scholars in this century have maintained that the life, death and resurrection of Jesus inaugurated the kingdom of God, producing an overlapping of the two ages. The kingdom has "already" dawned, but it is "not yet" complete. The first aspect pertains to Jesus' first coming, being attested to by such verses as Matthew 11:12; 12:28; Mark 1:15; 4:11; Luke 11:20; 17:21 and John 3:5. These passages speak of the reality that the age to come has dawned. The second aspect relates to Jesus' second coming, being attested to by verses like Luke 11:2; 22:29; 23:42; Mark 13:26 (compare Mt 24:30; Lk 21:27). These passages speak of the reality that this present age is still in operation. The result of these two perspectives is that the Christian lives in eschatological tension. That is to say, the kingdom of God rules in the hearts of the people of God, but within the context of this evil age.

Classical dispensationalists often assert that, with the Jews' rejection of Jesus, the kingdom of God was postponed until the parousia. However, the fact that the early church continued Jesus' message about the kingdom of God having dawned is devastating evidence against the postponed kingdom theory. Paul, too, shared in the belief of the dawning of the kingdom of God. In his writings one finds the "already/not yet" perspective on the kingdom. It has dawned (Rom 14:7; 1 Cor 4:20; 15:24; Col 1:13; 4:11) but, at the same time, it is not yet complete (1 Cor 6:9-10; 15:24, 50; Gal 5:21; Eph 5:5; 1 Thess 2:2; 2 Thess 1:5). Thus the kingdom of God began with Jesus in spiritual form through God's reign over the hearts of his people, but it awaits its physical and earthly manifestation until the parousia (Rev 20:1-6).

Judgment of the Righteous and the Wicked

The coming judgment is one of the most persistent and important themes in Jewish eschatology. At the end of history the divine sentence would be spoken over the righteous and the wicked, bringing reward to the former and condemnation to the latter (Dan 12:1-3; *1 Enoch* 10:8-9; *2 Enoch* 65:6; 4 Ezra 12:33-34; compare Mt 24:31-51; Mk 13:27; Lk 21:34-36; Rev 20:11-15). Two New Testament authors in particular, Paul and John, indicate that such judgment began with the first coming of Jesus.

Although Paul does not give extended treatment to the theme of judgment, it nevertheless is undeniably present in his writings (compare Dan 12:1-3; *1 Enoch* 10:8-9; *2 Enoch* 65:6; 4 Ezra 12:33-34), under two categories: the justification of the saved and wrath upon the lost. Once again the overlapping of the two ages is at work in the apostle's thinking. Regarding the saved, they have already been declared righteous in Christ and found to be not guilty (Rom 3:21-26; 5:1; 8:1, 33-34; 2 Cor 5:21; 1 Thess 1:10; 5:9). Yet, Christians still must appear before the judgment seat of Christ/God to have their works evaluated for rewards, or lack thereof (Rom 14:10; 1 Cor 3:12-15; 2 Cor 5:10; Gal 5:5; compare Rom 2:7, 10). This combination of futurist and realized eschatology also impacts the lost. They will appear one day before God to receive divine eternal wrath (Rom 2:5, 8, 19; 9:22), but this wrath has already begun to impinge upon their lives (Rom 1:18; 4:15; 1 Thess 2:16). There is, however, opportunity for the latter to join the ranks of the former, by faith in Christ (Eph 2:3).[40]

The second author who indicates that the end-time judgment began with the first coming of Jesus is John. While the Fourth Gospel contains references to a future judgment and resurrection (6:39-40, 44, 54; 7:37; 11:24; 12:48), the emphasis lies elsewhere, namely in the claim that eschatological expectations have become present reality. Thus eternal life "already" belongs to those who have placed their faith in Christ (3:15-16, 36; 6:47, 51, 58; 8:51-52; 11:24-26; 10:28). Similarly divine worship is a present possession for those who believe (1:12-13; 3:3-8; compare 1 John 3:1, 10; 5:21). Furthermore, the end-time resurrection has broken into history for Christians (5:25). On the other side of the ledger, the judgment of the world and the nonbeliever has impacted the present moment (3:19; 5:22-24, 27, 30-38; 9:39; 12:31-33; 14:30; 16:11). In other words, according to the Gospel of John, one's acceptance or rejection of Jesus projects the end-time judgment into the present moment. Thus, we see yet another sign associated with the end of history as having already dawned with the first coming of Christ.

The New Creation
The aspiration for a new creation runs deep in Judaism (Is 11:6-8; 65:17, 22; Ezek 34:25-27; *Jubilees* 1:29; *1 Enoch* 91:16; *Sibylline Oracles* 3.43, 431, 690; 4 Ezra 6:1-6; *2 Apocalypse of Baruch* 3:7; see also 2 Pet 3:10-13; compare Rev 21—22 with Gen 1—3). Although the complete fulfillment of that expectation is still future, the apostle Paul would surely have received the support of his New Testament colleagues with a statement like that found in 2 Corinthians 5:17, "Therefore, if anyone is in Christ, he is a new creation; the old has gone, the new has come!" In other words, in Christ the new creation has dawned.

Conclusion
It has been our aim to demonstrate that, in its equating of this current generation exclusively with the last generation, doomsday prophecy is theologically imbalanced. In particular, it misses one of the key messages of the New Testament—the signs of the times began with Jesus and his generation: the rise of the antichrist, the messianic woes, the kingdom of God, the judgment of the righteous and wicked, and the new creation. Grasping this perspective delivers one from confining this or that generation to the last days, especially since they (the last days) have been in progress almost two thousand years and could continue for another two thousand years before Jesus returns.

3
This Generation Will Not Pass Away
Doomsday Prophecy & the Key Biblical Texts

IN THIS CHAPTER WE EXAMINE FIVE SCRIPTURAL PASSAGES COMmonly appealed to by doomsday preachers in support of their prophetic calendar of events: (1) Genesis 15:18: Did Israel's return to its land in 1948 begin the fulfillment of the Abrahamic covenant? (2) Ezekiel 38—39: Will Russia invade Israel at the end of time? (3) Daniel 2, 7: Will the antichrist rule over a revived Roman Empire? (4) Daniel 9:24-27: Is Daniel's seventieth week imminent? (5) Mark 13:30: Are we living in the last generation? We will discover that, however sincerely motivated, the doomsday approach inadequately interprets these texts. The end-time superstructure the doomsday preachers build on these passages thus collapses.

Did Israel's Return to Its Land in 1948 Begin the Fulfillment of the Abrahamic Covenant? (Genesis 15:18)
The Abrahamic covenant, particularly as expressed in Genesis 15:18,

is critical for assessing the relationship between Israel and its land. That text says: "On that day the LORD made a covenant with Abram and said, 'To your descendants I give this land, from the river of Egypt to the great river, the Euphrates.' "

Recognizing the importance of this passage, the New Scofield Reference Bible (1967) supplies an interesting comment on Genesis 15:18, "The gift of the land is modified by prophecies of three dispossessions and restorations. . . . Two dispossessions and restorations have been accomplished. Israel is now in the third dispersion from which she will be restored at the return of the Lord as king under the Davidic Covenant" (p. 24).

While we agree with the general sentiments of these statements (especially the belief that the Abrahamic covenant as stated in Genesis 15:18 will one day be fulfilled by a permanent restoration of Israel to its land), it is the specifics which we contest. Particularly, we disagree that the twentieth century has necessarily witnessed the beginning of the third, and final, restoration of Israel to its rightful land. We hope and pray that Israel is permanently resettled in its land, but there are no Scriptural assurances that, as of 1948, Israel did in fact begin to fulfill Genesis 15:18. This issue demands more attention than space permits here, but two controversial questions call for comment at this juncture: (1) Was the Abrahamic covenant conditional or unconditional? (2) Has the Abrahamic covenant been fulfilled already?

First, is the Abrahamic covenant conditional or unconditional? Robert B. Chisholm pinpoints the issue involved in this question:

Those debating the millennial question disagree over the nature and eschatological implications of the Abrahamic covenant. On the one hand, many premillennialists, regarding the Abrahamic covenant as foundational to their system, have argued that God's promises to Abraham are unconditional and will be fulfilled literally through the nation Israel. On the other hand, amillennialists and postmillennialists have generally denied the unconditionality of the Abrahamic covenant and/or argued that its promises are fully realized only through the church, Abraham's spiritual offspring.[1]

Obviously, the vast majority of prophetic date setters align themselves with the first of these options (premillennialism), and they usually go on to argue that the Abrahamic covenant, unconditional as it is in nature, began to be fulfilled with Israel's "final" return to its land in 1948. While we wholeheartedly agree with the first of these conclusions (that the Abrahamic covenant is unconditional[2] and will one day be fulfilled literally through the nation Israel), it is a non sequitur to assume that the second conclusion is true (that that promise began to be fulfilled in 1948). The reason for this will become clear when we provide an answer to the second question.

Second, has the Abrahamic covenant been fulfilled? Here we have to avoid two extremes. Entrenched classical dispensationalists answer this question emphatically in the negative, asserting that the borders of Israel as delineated in Genesis 15:18 (the River of Egypt to the River Euphrates[3]) have never been realized. Only with Israel's ingathering in 1948 was the stage set for the imminent actualization of the prophecy. However, this assertion flies in the face of passages like 1 Kings 4:21, 24 and 2 Chronicles 9:26, which explicitly state that the Solomonic empire encompassed the territorial extent of Genesis 15:18. Attempts to deny the import of those passages by saying that Solomon only collected tribute money from the foreign kings within his domain but did not rule over their land are clearly begging the question. In ancient times, one did not collect money from a ruler unless one controlled that ruler, his people and his land. Covenantalists, on the other hand, answer this question emphatically in the affirmative, claiming that the scope of the Abrahamic covenant does not go beyond the Solomonic period. However, that is to overlook the fact that Genesis 17:7, 13, 19 explicitly states that the Abrahamic covenant is *eternal.* Other covenantalists recognize the eternality and the unconditionality of the Abrahamic covenant but proceed to apply its ultimate fulfillment to the church. After a careful consideration of the matter, Chisholm, rightly in our opinion, concludes:

> Establishing the unconditional nature of God's oath to Abraham does not necessarily entail a literal fulfillment of its promises through ethnic Israel living in an eschatological kingdom centered in the land of Canaan. For example, some amillennialists, while

agreeing that the promises are unconditional, find their fulfillment exclusively in the church. While the church, as Abraham's spiritual offspring, does inherit God's promises to the patriarch and participate to some degree in their fulfillment, this does not preclude a literal eschatological realization of the promises through ethnic Israel. The writers of the OT, including those living in the postexilic period, and the apostle Paul anticipated such a literal fulfillment.[4] We agree with this assessment of the data and would hasten to add, however, that there is no biblical hint that the *final* fulfillment of the Abrahamic covenant began in 1948. Rather, we suspect that that prophecy, like other end-time Scriptural prophecies, finds multiple fulfillments in history (in this case one fulfillment of Gen 15:18 occurs in 1 Kings 4:21, 24/2 Chron 9:26). If that is so, then who is to say that there will not be future displacements and restorations of Israel to her rightful land long after 1948?

Will Russia Invade Israel at the End of Time? (Ezekiel 38—39)

Until the recent demise of the Soviet Union, it was fashionable for gloom-and-doom preachers to predict an end-time invasion of Israel by the Soviet Union, based on a *pesher*-like interpretation of Ezekiel 38—39. Those chapters speak of a foe from the North sweeping down on Israel, apparently in a time of peace and security, with the express purpose of destroying and then plundering it. But, according to Ezekiel, it is actually God who lures Israel's enemies against it, so that he can destroy them, thereby displaying his power and glory and love for Israel.

Who is the foe from the North and when will it attack Israel? Ezekiel identifies Israel's enemy as Gog of the land of Magog, the chief prince of Meshech and Tubal (Ezek 38:1). According to many doomsday preachers, Gog and Magog denote the Russians, Rosh (chief prince) is Russia, Meshech is Moscow, and Tubal is Tobolsk.[5] Based on this identification, this approach goes on to argue that halfway through the seven-year Tribulation period, after Israel has signed a peace pact with the antichrist (the head of the ten-nation European Common Market), thus accounting for Israel's state of peace in the land, Russia will invade Israel from the North in its last bid for world conquest. However, God will intervene on behalf of his people the Jews and destroy the Russian army. So great will be Russia's destruction that the clean-up operation in the aftermath of the invasion will take seven months. In fact, the fuel from Russia's weapons (nuclear?) will burn for seven years!

What are we to make of this intriguing and foreboding hypothesis? Three arguments combine to question it: grammatical, geographical and etymological.

First, on grammatical grounds, taking the Hebrew term *rōʾš* as a proper name is debatable (and even more so if the proper name, *rōʾš*, is then equated with Russia). To be sure, some translations follow that approach (the Jerusalem Bible, the New English Bible and the New American Standard Bible). However, another way to render the term is as a generic noun—"chief" or "head" prince (as does the King James Version, the Revised Standard Version, the New American Bible and the New International Version). The resulting translation is as follows: "Son of Man, set your face against Gog, the land of Magog, the *chief* prince of Meshech and Tubal. . . ." On this reading *rōʾš* is the head of, not a part of the series of, Meshech and Tubal.

Second, from a geographical perspective, one of the primary reasons doomsday prophets equate Russia with the invading foe is because the Soviet Union lies directly north of Israel. But, as archaeologist Barry Beitzel observes, the basic way for an enemy to attack ancient Israel, which lay at the bottom of the fertile crescent, was from the North, regardless of where the foe resided.[6] Beitzel writes:

> Accordingly, the Bible's use of the expression "north" denotes the direction from which a foe would normally approach and not the location of its homeland. The implications of this observation are especially important when interpreting some of the eschatological narratives within the Old Testament prophets.[7]

Third, further damaging to the theory of the equation of the enemy from the North with the Soviet Union is the etymological evidence. Historian Edwin Yamauchi notes that, even if one transliterated the Hebrew *rōʾš* as a proper name (as the Septuagint does), it can have nothing to do with modern Russia. Yamauchi writes, "This would be a gross anachronism, for the modern name is based upon the name *Rus,* which was brought into the reign of Kiev, north of the Black Sea, by the Vikings only in the Middle Ages."[8] Yamauchi goes on to analyze the nomenclature "Gog and Magog" and reaches the majority scholarly opinion, namely, that we simply cannot positively identify the antecedents of these historical names.[9] However, the identifications of *Meshech* and *Tubal* are not in doubt. Few scholars today equate them with Moscow and Tobolsk. Rather, combined ancient testimony attests to the fact that Meshech and Tubal were located in central and eastern Anatolia (Asia Minor), respectively.[10]

The foregoing arguments render the "Russian" hypothesis untenable. This is not to deny, however, that, based on a historical incident occurring approximately at the time of Ezekiel, the prophet[11] used that event as a picture or foreshadowing of an end-time invasion of Israel. If so, it would once again illustrate the biblical authors' propensity to use the eschatological-prophetic hermeneutic, of casting future events in terms of present experience. In this particular case, however, interpreters cannot as yet be certain of the identification of either.

Will the Antichrist Rule over a Revived Roman Empire? (Daniel 2 and 7)

It is a common assumption among doomsday preachers that, based on passages like Daniel 2 and 7, the end times will witness a revival of the Roman Empire over which the antichrist will rule. In looking for a modern entity which fulfills the prophecy of a revived Roman Empire, one need look no further than the European Common Market. Malgo's comments typify this understanding:

> This means that Jesus' coming in lowliness at Bethlehem and His second coming in great power and glory will take place in the world empire and amongst the same people. Under which regime was He born? Under the Roman regime. For this reason the Lord can only come when the Roman empire has been established, and this is taking place now. . . . The European Common Market and the Euraton date back to two contracts which were signed in Rome in

the year 1957 by Belgium, France, Holland, Italy, Luxembourg and West Germany. . . . England has also fallen into the trap, and the Scandinavian countries too. . . . Daniel 2 and 7 clearly say that this alliance of ten nations will appear on the world stage. When? Immediately before the return of the Lord Jesus. We are living at this time right now. . . . United Europe, the re-established Roman Empire, must be a very powerful bloc. How will this be achieved? It will be welded together through political, economic, and religious unity and at its head will be the great strong man, the Antichrist.[12]

The deductive logic is clear in all of this—the European Common Market is the fulfillment of the revived Roman Empire which is predicted in the Bible as occurring in the last generation. But is such reasoning accurate? Does the Bible predict that the ancient Roman Empire will be revived at the end of history? If not, then the doom-and-gloom equation of the European Common Market and a revived Roman Empire is miscalculated. The key Scriptures in the formula appealed to by doomsday prophets are Daniel 2 and 7, especially the identification of the fourth kingdom therein. We will briefly summarize these two passages, providing a more viable alternative to the current interpretation espoused by Malgo and others.

Although Daniel 2 and 7 record two separate dreams (Dan 2—the dream of Nebuchadnezzar; Dan 7—Daniel's dream), they deal with the same scenario—the unfolding in history of four powerful kingdoms, beginning with Daniel's day.[13] There are two basic approaches today toward identifying these four kingdoms. Many interpreters (including doomsday preachers) argue for the following:

Kingdom	Leader	Date
1. Babylonian	Nebuchadnezzar	ca. 570 B.C.
2. Medo-Persian	Cyrus	ca. 539 B.C.
3. Greek	Alexander the Great	ca. 330 B.C.
4. Revived Roman Empire	Antichrist	In the end-time

It becomes obvious from the chart that the doomsday prediction of a revived Roman Empire turns on the identification of the fourth kingdom. However, a more widely accepted interpretation of the fourth kingdom exists:

Kingdom	Leader	Date
1. Babylonian	Nebuchadnezzar	ca. 570 B.C.
2. Media	Astyages	ca. 550 B.C.
3. Persian	Cyrus	ca. 539 B.C.
4. Greek	Alexander the Great	ca. 330 B.C.

On this reading, the fourth kingdom is Greece, not a revived Roman Empire. Moreover, this kingdom already occurred in history, and therefore it does not call for an exclusively futuristic interpretation. In other words, if the fourth kingdom was Greece, then the modern-day doomsday equation of a revived Roman Empire (ruled by the antichrist) and the European Common Market turns out to be unscriptural. In what follows, we will summarize the evangelical expression of the second approach, briefly correlating the biblical descriptions of the four kingdoms with the historical data.[14]

Concerning the identification of the first kingdom in Daniel 2 and 7 there is no debate. The head of the statue made of fine gold, the most valuable of metals (Dan 2:32, 37-38) and the lion with the wings of an eagle, an ancient symbol for Babylon (Dan 7:4),[15] by consensus, represent the Babylonian kingdom under king Nebuchadnezzar.

It is with the second kingdom that the problem of identification surfaces. A large number of conservatives (doomsday prophets included) interpret the chest and arms of silver on the human statue (Dan 2:32) and the bear with three ribs in its mouth (Dan 7:5) as the Medo-Persian Empire led by Cyrus, who conquered Babylon in 539 B.C. This is understandable since that empire came to rule over three nations—Lydia, Babylon and Egypt (the three ribs). However, other conservatives such as Gurney and Walton make a very plausible case for identifying the second kingdom with the Median Empire alone. That kingdom, under the leadership of the likes of Astyages (550 B.C.) and Cyaxares II, also defeated three nations—Urartu, Mannaea and the Scythians.[16]

Two pieces of evidence tip the scales in favor of the latter interpretation. First, identifying the three ribs in the bear's mouth with Urartu, Mannaea and the Scythians corresponds with Jeremiah 51:27-29. That passage speaks of three nations joining the Medes against Babylon—

Ararat, Minni and Ashkenaz, which respectively represent Urartu, Mannaea and the Scythians.[17] All three of these peoples were defeated by the Medes and were incorporated into its empire. The second piece of evidence is that the inferiority of the second empire when compared to the first (Babylonia, Dan 2:39) fits Media much more readily than Medo-Persia.

The only real problem with this view is that little is known about the Median Empire. However, Walton aptly responds to this difficulty:

One of the difficulties here is that we know so little of the Median empire. Its territory was roughly similar to the size of the Neo-Babylonian empire. During the rule of Nebuchadnezzar's successors the Median monarch was Astyages (585-550). There can be little question of Astyages' influence, for he married one of his daughters to Nebuchadnezzar, while the other was married to Cambyses I of Persia and became the mother of Cyrus. Even Nebuchadnezzar's fear of Median power is evidenced in the fortifications he built along the northern frontier. Both Elam and Susa seem to have fallen prey to Astyages' expansion after the death of Nebuchadnezzar. All of this would give historical support to the view that Media may have been considered a world empire that succeeded Babylon in power after the death of Nebuchadnezzar, though the city of Babylon had not yet fallen.[18]

The third kingdom, the belly and thighs of bronze in the human statue (Dan 2:32, 39) and the leopard with four wings and four heads (Dan 7:6), is equated by doomsday prophets (and many evangelical interpreters) with Alexander the Great (the leopard) and the four generals who divided Alexander's kingdom among themselves upon his death (323 B.C.). Those four generals were: Cassander (the West—Greece), Lysimachus (the North—Asia), Seleucius (the East—Babylonia and Syria) and Ptolemy (the South— Egypt).

This view is reasonable, but an alternate approach, and one that is just as viable, is that the third kingdom represents the Persian Empire. On this reading, the leopard represents Persia, which, with the brilliant, swift-moving armies of Cyrus, defeated the ponderous, bearlike Median empire.[19] The four wings and four heads could signify the four corners of the universe, corresponding to Persia's world domination (contrasted to Media's more limited influence). Or they might just as well symbolize the four Persian kings known to Scripture: Cyrus, Artaxerxes, Xerxes and Darius III Codomannus (who was defeated by Alexander the Great). Furthermore, as Gurney points out, the marked superiority of the third kingdom over the second (Dan 2:39; 7:6) better fits Persian supremacy over the inferior Median Empire than Greece's relationship to Persia, since both the latter were world powers.[20] Moreover, Gurney goes on to observe that the four successors to Alexander, both in history and in Daniel 8, represent diluted strength, whereas in Daniel 7 the four heads/wings seem to represent the strength itself.[21]

The identification of the fourth kingdom in Daniel 2 and 7 with the Roman Empire has a long history, going back to New Testament times (*2 Apocalypse of Baruch* 39:1-18 [A.D. 90]; 4 Ezra 12:10-12 [A.D. 80]; Josephus [*Antiquities of the Jews* 10.11.7]; the Talmud [*b. Šebu'ot* 20; *b. 'Aboda Zara* 26, second to fifth centuries A.D.]; Irenaeus; Hippolytus; Origen).[22] The doomsday prophets have not failed to exploit this interpretation for their own purpose, namely, to argue for a revived Roman Empire in the end time. However, the identification of Daniel's fourth kingdom with Greece, as led by Alexander the Great, also has a venerable history of interpretation, going back even *before* New Testament times to Herodotus (1.95.130; 300 B.C.) and the *Sibylline Oracles*, book 4 (140 B.C.), and continuing with Roman historians at the time of the New Testament (Tacitus *Historiae* 5.8-9; Dionysius of Halicarnassus 1.2.1; Appianus *Introduction to Roman History*).

We proceed now to summarize the two preceding interpretations of the fourth kingdom, taking special notice of Daniel 2:40-43 and 7:19-24. The doomsday mentality applies these passages to Rome, appealing to the following pieces of evidence: (1) The Roman Empire fits the description of being a beast, unlike the three earlier empires, primarily because of its unsurpassed power (it was like iron—Dan 2:40; compare 7:19). According to the doomsday approach, this was the first stage of the Roman Empire, occurring in approximately 167 B.C. (2) Accordingly, Daniel 7:20 catapults the reader forward in time to, in effect, the twentieth century A.D., with its description of the ten horns and the one horn which emerges out of the ten with uncontested power. This is the second phase of the Roman Empire, the revival of the Roman Empire, soon to be constituted as the ten nations of the European Common Market and eventually to be led by the antichrist.

This viewpoint has been wildly popular among contemporary Christians, but it is without solid basis. Two formidable problems militate against equating the fourth kingdom with the revived Roman Empire. First, this viewpoint, without explanation, assumes that Daniel 7:20 suddenly jumps ahead in time from Daniel's day to the twentieth century, even though there is no indication of this in the text.

Second, this interpretation departs from the hermeneutic long cherished by evangelicals since the Reformation by failing to root the biblical text in its historical-cultural environment. Had this route been taken, it would have been seen that the Greek Empire beautifully explains Daniel 2:40-43 and 7:19-24. The following summary utilizes that background. Daniel 2:40, 7:7 and 7:19 declare that the fourth kingdom will be like iron, crushing all its opponents, a fitting description of Alexander the Great's army, which was totally invincible in the face of its foes, whereas Rome was stopped by Parthia in its attempted expansion.[23] Daniel 7:23 tells us that the fourth kingdom will be unlike the previous three kingdoms. The Western civilization of Greece was very different from the three Oriental empires of Babylonia, Media and Persia, whereas Rome was in many ways similar to Greece.[24] Daniel 2:40-43 asserts that the fourth kingdom will be divided into two parts, iron and clay, which will not mix well together, a perfect analysis of the Seleucid kingdom (Syria, the stronger part, iron) and the Ptolemaic (Egypt, the weaker part, the clay, which was eventually overrun by the Seleucids). The reference to the two substances not mixing together distinctly reminds one of the rupture between the two kingdoms, which occurred despite the intermarriage between them.[25] We read in Daniel 7:20, 24 that the fourth kingdom will divide into ten horns or kingdoms, which Walton convincingly identifies with the ten independent states (third century B.C.) that eventually replaced the four territories of the four generals who succeeded Alexander the great—Ptolemaic Egypt, Seleucia, Macedon, Pergamum, Pontus, Bithynia, Cappadocia, Armenia, Parthia and Bactria.[26] Two of these surface in the biblical narrative because of their relevance to Israel in the second century B.C.—Seleucia and Ptolemaic Egypt, as we have seen (Dan 2:40-43). Finally, Daniel 7:8, 20-22, 24-25, with its description of the one horn gaining supremacy over three of the other horns (kings), as Walton argues, is nicely explained by the defeat of Cappadocia, Armenia and Parthia by Antiochus the Great (second century B.C.), whose infamous son, Antiochus Epiphanes, continued his father's exploits and severely persecuted the Jews. Walton explains the father-son relationship with regard to Daniel's "little horn":

> While the subduing of the three horns then makes excellent sense in connection with Antiochus the Great, we are faced with the problem that he does not qualify as a convincing little horn with regard to the remainder of the description given in Daniel. That distinction still would seem to suit Antiochus Epiphanes better.
>
> A hypothesis that would take advantage of the strengths of each of these elements is one that would see the incorporation of Palestine into the Seleucid state under Antiochus the Great as the beginning of the kingdom of the little horn, which would then be continued and brought to culmination under Antiochus Epiphanes. It is true that Dan 7:24 speaks of the little horn as a king rather than a kingdom, but we should notice that even in that context (7:17) the two are seen to be interchangeable.[27]

Is Daniel's Seventieth Week Imminent? (Daniel 9:24-27)

The late J. A. Montgomery once said of Daniel 9:24-27, "The history of the exegesis of the 70 weeks is the Dismal Swamp of OT criticism."[28] Recently, Michael Kalafian has helpfully surveyed the history of interpretation of this text, dividing it into three major views: the premillennial interpretation, the amillennial interpretation and the higher critical, or liberal, interpretation.[29] The critical issue involves locating in time the threefold periodization delineated in Daniel 9:24-27: the first unit of seven "sevens" or forty-nine years, the second unit of sixty-two "sevens," or 434 years; and the last seven or seven years. The total period is seventy "sevens" or 490 years. The following chart encapsulates the three views:

Views	1st Unit: 49 Years ("7 Weeks")	2nd Unit: 434 Years ("62 weeks")	3rd Unit: 7 Years ("1 Week")
1. Premillennial	445 B.C. (Artaxerxes' decree to rebuild Jerusalem)	Completed in A.D. 33 with the death of Jesus Christ (allowing for leap years and a 360-day year)[30]	Long gap after 69th week (church age), then 70th week = 7-year Tribulation with antichrist in control
2. Amillennial	445 B.C. (Artaxerxes' decree to rebuild Jerusalem)	Completed in A.D. 33 with the death of Christ	Short gap after 69th week (the death of Christ), then 70th week = A.D. 70 destruction of Jerusalem
3. Liberal	587 B.C. (beginning of Babylonian captivity) to 538 B.C. (Joshuae the high priest)	605 B.C. (date of Jeremiah's prophecy) to 171 B.C. (murder of High Priest, Onias III)	171 B.C. (Antiochus Epiphanes' persecution of the Jews) to 164 B.C. (the restoration of the temple)

The first interpretation has supplied fodder for the prophetic agenda of the doomsday prophets, in that the common assumption of such preachers is that with Israel's restoration to its rightful land in 1948, Daniel's seventieth week is now poised, ready to strike, waiting only for the rapture of the church. The scene is set: Israel was reestablished as a nation in 1948, as prophesied in Ezekiel 38—39; Russia has become a world power, again according to Ezekiel 38—39; the revived Roman Empire has arisen in fulfillment of Daniel 2 and 7, in the form of the European Common Market. The prophecy clock which will tick away the last generation has begun. Based on these assumptions, the gloom-and-doom messengers believe that the seventieth week of Daniel is imminent.

However, there is a fatal flaw in the hermeneutic of this approach—it allegorizes Daniel 9:24-27 and, in so doing, overlooks the historical fact that Daniel's prophecy has already been fulfilled, not in A.D. 1948, but in 164 B.C.! Assuming that to be the case, there is no biblical reason why 1948 necessarily began the last generation. Although we believe that Israel's return to its land in that year was providential, it may or may not be eschatological. If Daniel 9:24-27 has already been fulfilled, then equating the current generation exclusively with the time of Christ's return is not justifiable. As we saw regarding Genesis 15:18 and 2 Chronicles 9:8 and 26, the promise to Abraham has already been fulfilled and, as we understand it, will be fulfilled again (see Rom 11:25-27). The same thing can be said of Daniel 9:24-27. Actually, comparing Daniel 9:24-27 with the Olivet Discourse of Jesus suggests that the events of Daniel's prophecy involve *three* fulfillments. We seek to develop this thesis in what follows. The bulk of our investigation will center on Daniel 9:24-27.

While none of the three views delineated regarding Daniel 9:24-27 is without difficulty, it seems to us that the third view is the most accurate exegesis of that text. Although commonly called the liberal approach, the third view need not be associated with higher criticism, especially if one holds to the Danielic authorship of the book. On this reading, Daniel's supernatural prophecy uttered during the Babylonian exile of the Jews in the sixth century B.C. was precisely fulfilled in later history. Accordingly, we proceed to explain Daniel 9:24-27 following the evangelical hermeneutic—the historical, cultural and grammatical method. Our analysis of the passage is based on the Revised Standard Version, because we believe it most accurately translates the Hebrew text.

9:24: *"Seventy weeks of years are decreed concerning your people and your holy city, to finish the transgression, to put an end to sin, and to atone for iniquity, to bring in everlasting righteousness, to seal both vision and prophet, and to anoint a most holy place."*

Daniel 9 records Daniel's prayer of repentance on behalf of himself and Israel. According to 9:2, Daniel was meditating on the prophecy of Jeremiah (Jer 25:11; 29:10) that forecast a period of seventy years for the Jews' captivity in Babylon. With the rise of Darius the Mede in 538 B.C., Daniel became concerned about the time of the fulfillment of Jeremiah's prophecy. In response to his prayer, the angel Gabriel appeared to him and reinterpreted the seventy years of captivity, expanding them into seventy sevens, or 490 years (9:22-24). According to verse 24, by the time the seventy sevens end, six things are to be achieved for Jerusalem. The first three have to do with God's eventual forgiveness of Israel's sin: "finish the transgression," "put an end to sin" and "atone for iniquity." The second three are the positive counterparts to the first three: the bringing in of righteousness, the vindication of the prophet and the anointing of the holy place.

Although it is often asserted that the six items in Daniel 9:24 have not yet been fulfilled, in one sense all of the aforementioned prophecies were partially realized in the Maccabean era. This is especially noticeable in connection with Judas Maccabeus's rededication of the Jerusalem temple in 164 B.C., after its desecration by Antiochus Epiphanes in 167 B.C. One should compare Daniel 8:13-14 with Daniel 9:24 in this regard. Comparing Daniel 9:24 and Daniel 8 leads Goldingay to comment:

> A coherent understanding of v. 24 emerges, then, if we take it as a restatement of the visionary promises of chap. 8. Like that vision, it looks forward from the time of Daniel himself to the Antiochene crisis, and promises God's deliverance. There is no reason to refer it exegetically to the first or second coming of Christ.[31]

9:25: *"Know therefore and understand that from the going forth of the word to restore and build Jerusalem to the coming of an anointed one, a prince, there shall be seven weeks. Then for sixty-two weeks it shall be built again with squares and moat, but in a troubled time."*

Verse 25 delineates two time units—the first seven weeks of years (49 years) and the next sixty-two weeks of years (434 years). The typical doomsday interpretation of this text is that it refers to Artaxerxes' decree in 445 B.C. to rebuild Jerusalem (before the first week of sevens or 49 years), while the prince, the Messiah, is Jesus, whose death in A.D. 33 completed the 434 years (the sixty-two weeks of sevens). However, there are two insurmountable problems with this view. First, the term used to describe the rebuilding of Jerusalem is not "decree," but "word" *(dābār),* in particular a prophetic word. Thus, it is not the decree of the Persian king Artaxerxes, but the predictive word of the Lord through *Jeremiah* in 587 B.C. that Jerusalem would one day be restored (Jer 30:18-22; 31:38-40) that Daniel refers to here. Second, the doomsday preachers are clearly fudging when they translate the Hebrew word *māšîaḥ* as "the Messiah" (Jesus). In fact, the Hebrew has no definite article and should be rendered, "an anointed one," a term that could even be applied to a pagan king such as Cyrus, the Persian (Is 45:1). The next word, *nāgîd,* can refer to a prince (e.g., 1 Sam 2:10, 35; 9:16; 10:1) or a (high) priest (e.g., Lev 4:3; Jer 20:1; Neh 11:11). Adding forty-nine years to the time of Jeremiah's prophetic word in 587 B.C. leaves no doubt about who that "anointed one" was—it was Joshua, the high priest, who came to Jerusalem in 538 B.C. with Governor Zerubbabel for the purpose of rebuilding Jerusalem.

Continuing our interpretation of verse 25, we believe the next time unit—sixty-two weeks of sevens (434 years)—is to be identified as the period extending from 605 B.C. (the date of the oracle in Jer 25:1, 11 about the coming destruction of Jerusalem) to 171 B.C. (the year of the murder of Onias III; see the comments that follow on v. 26). The interpretation appealed to by the doomsday preacher combines the 49 years with the 434 years into one unit (483 years) in order to arrive at a fulfillment date of A.D. 33 (the death of Jesus Christ). However, the Hebrew text as we have it does not permit this rendering, because it separates the 49 years from the 434 years with a punctuation mark. Thus, the two units are probably not consecutive. Rather, because the two units are separated and not added together, we are permitted to view the second unit (434 years) as overlapping or concurrent with the first unit (49 years). The beginning of the second unit is best identified as 605 B.C., the time of Jeremiah's prophecy about Israel's destruction (Jer 25:1, 11). Subtracting 434 years from 605 B.C. leads one to 171 B.C., the precise date of the murder of Onias III.[32]

9:26: *"And after the sixty-two weeks, an anointed one shall be cut off, and shall have nothing; and the people of the prince who is to come shall destroy the city and the sanctuary. Its end shall come with a flood, and to the end there shall be war; desolations are decreed."*

Two personages appear on the scene at the end of the 62 weeks of seven (434 years), an anointed one who is cut off and a prince who brings war and sacrilege on Jerusalem and its temple. The first undoubtedly refers to the righteous Zadokite high priest, Onias III, who was murdered in 171 B.C. by the order of Menelaus, the wicked priest appointed by Antiochus Epiphanes. The second personage is Antiochus Epiphanes, that Seleucid king who began persecuting the Jews in 171 B.C., trying to force them to give up their faith and to accept Greek religion in its place. The havoc he wrought on Jerusalem is described at length in 1 Maccabees 1—4 and 2 Maccabees 4—5.

9:27: *"And he shall make a strong covenant with many for one week; and for half of the week he shall cause sacrifice and offering to cease; and upon the wing of abominations shall come one who makes desolate, until the decreed end is poured out on the desolator."*

Daniel's seventieth week (seven years) began in 171 B.C. with Antiochus's murder of Onias III and his persecution of Jerusalem, and continued until 164 B.C. At first, Antiochus, the Gentile, made a covenant with Hellenistically inclined Jews (Dan 11:30; compare 1 Maccabees 1:11). However, halfway through the week (about three and one-half years later, 168-164 B.C.; compare Dan 8:11; 11:31; 1 Maccabees 1:29-64), Antiochus decreed that the temple sacrifices and offerings cease. To add insult to injury, he profaned the holy of holies by placing in it a statue to Zeus (the chief Greek god) and then sacrificing to Zeus a pig on the altar there (described in Dan 9:27 as "winged" or horned altar). This terrible action is referred to as the abomination of desolation, "and upon the wings of abominations shall come one who makes desolate." This happened in 167 B.C. However, Daniel 9:27 promises that the desolator (Antiochus) would be defeated, which, in fact, occurred in 164 B.C., when Judas Maccabeus led a Jewish revolt that expelled the Seleucid ruler from Jerusalem. He then rededicated the temple to Yahweh in December 164 B.C., celebrated today as Hanukkah (compare 1 Maccabees 4:36-61).

So we see, then, that the prediction of Daniel 9:24-27 came true. But was there more significance to that prophecy than its fulfillment during the Maccabean period? According to the Olivet Discourse there was. Based on Matthew 24:15 and Mark 13:14, a second fulfillment of the Danielic prophecy came true when Titus, the Roman general, ransacked Jerusalem and destroyed the Jewish temple. And, according to Luke 21:20-28 (compare 2 Thess 2:1-11 [especially v. 4]), the Danielic prophecy will apparently be fulfilled a third time, when the antichrist will be fully and finally manifested. However, for our purpose, we bring this section to a close by noting that, in light of the historical fulfillments of Daniel 9:24-27 (but without denying its future significance either) we may now answer the question, Is Daniel's seventieth week imminent? Not necessarily. That being the case, we need not lock Jesus' return in to this present generation.

Are We Living in the Last Generation? (Mark 13:30)
We are left with a final text often appealed to by doomsday prophets in support of their view that 1948 began the last generation and that Jesus will therefore return by A.D. 2000—Mark 13:30, "This generation will certainly not pass away until all these things have happened" (compare Mt 24:34 and Lk 21:32). Actually, their interpretation of this passage is but one of five views concerning Mark 13:30: (1) the reconstitution of Israel as a nation in 1948 began the fulfillment of this passage (the doomsday approach); (2) the generation Jesus referred to was the end-time generation, whenever that may be; (3) the words *hē genea hautē* mean "this nation" or "this race," and therefore Jesus was saying that the Jewish people as a race will not perish; (4) Jesus referred to his own generation as the people who would witness the parousia; (5) Jesus referred to his contemporaries as the generation that would experience the fall of Jerusalem, which happened in A.D. 70. As we describe these views, we will see that the last one appears to be the most probable.

As we said, doomsday preachers and writers adamantly argue that the reconstitution of Israel as a nation in 1948 began the fulfillment of Mark 13:30. Hal Lindsey spearheads this viewpoint. Referring to Mark 13:28-30, he believes that the infallible sign of the time, Israel, is "the fig tree" of Jesus' parable and that, on May 14, 1948, it put out its first leaves. Concerning Jesus' statement that "this generation" would not pass away until all had taken place, Lindsey tantalizingly comments:

What generation? Obviously, in context, the generation that would see the signs—chief among them the rebirth of Israel. A generation in the Bible is something like forty years. If this is a correct deduction, then within forty years or so of 1948, all these things could take place. Many scholars who have studied Bible prophecy all their lives believe that this is so.[33]

The second view of Mark 13:30 is that Jesus speaks therein about the end-time generation. That is, that generation which happens to be alive when the signs of the times delineated in the Olivet Discourse take place will witness the return of Christ.

The third view argues that the words *hē genea hautē* refer to the Jewish race. Accordingly, Jesus was promising that throughout time, even in those last days in which the signs of the times occur, God will providentially protect his people, the Jews, from extermination. While we too believe that God will sustain and deliver the Jewish people throughout the course of history and one day will permanently restore them to their land, we do not think the translation "race" or "nation" properly renders the Markan phrase. In fact, the words *hē genea hautē* elsewhere in Mark are consistently translated "this generation," referring to Jesus' contemporaries (Mk 8:12, 38; 9:19). It undoubtedly requires the same rendering in Mark 13:30.

The fourth view states that Jesus was saying that "all these things" (the signs of the times) would lead to his return before his generation passed away. This approach bluntly asserts that Jesus was mistaken, because the parousia did not occur at that time.

In our opinion, the fatal flaw in all of these interpretations is their failure to accurately identify the antecedent of the words "these things." Those following the first view interpret these words as referring to the signs of the times initiated in 1948, when Israel became a nation. The second view, a commendable approach, nevertheless fails to distinguish the "these things" (signs of the times) of the fall of Jerusalem in A.D. 70 from the parousia. We have already discounted the third view's translation of *hē genea hautē* as "nation" or "race." The fourth view, the liberal approach, like the second, fails to distinguish the signs of the times of the fall of Jerusalem in A.D. 70 from the parousia. The primary difference between these two perspectives is that the second view projects both events into the future, preserving Jesus' prophetic accuracy, while the fourth view retrojects the predicted fulfillment of both events into the past at the time of Jesus' generation. However the nonoccurrence of the parousia at that time discredits Jesus' prophetic ability. We find this view to be particularly unacceptable.

The fifth view is the only approach that properly relates the words "these things" to the parousia, thereby providing the intended meaning of "this generation." The signs of the times ("these things") Jesus referred to were the events surrounding the fall of Jerusalem in A.D. 70. A. L. Moore ably defends this perspective on Mark 13:30.[34] He bases his approach on two points, one grammatical and the other contextual.

Grammatically, a number of interpreters think that the phrase "all these things" *(tauta panta)* in verse 30 refers to the signs of the times immediately preceding the parousia. But against this assumption is the fact that "all these things" of verse 30 refers back to the "these things" mentioned in verse 29, which refers to the events preceding the end, but *not* the end itself. In effect, verses 29-30 speak of the signs of the times that would lead up to the *fall of Jerusalem* in A.D. 70 (vv. 14-23), not the parousia, which were precisely fulfilled in Jesus' generation.[35]

The aforementioned argument is confirmed, according to Moore, by the contextual evidence, that is, the structure of the Olivet Discourse. Moore outlines the passage like this:

vv. 1-4	Introduction. The question raised in v. 4 leading to a discourse on the end and its date, and the signs of the end and their dates.
vv. 5-23	The signs of the end enframed at either end by warnings against the seduction of false messiahs and prophets with the fictitious claim (vv. 5-6 and 21-23).
vv. 24-27	The end itself.
vv. 28-31	Regarding the time of the signs of the end, and their significance for perceiving the time of the end itself.
vv. 32-37	Regarding the time of the end event.[36]

From this structure one can detect that a parallel theme emerges— the signs of the times seem to be separated from the parousia:

Signs of the Times	Parousia
1. vv. 5-23	vv. 24-27
2. vv. 28-31	vv. 32-37

Moore's conclusion seems justified, "Whereas the signs will occur within the immediate future (though not necessarily exhausted by that immediate future), the end itself is not so delimited."[37] Moore's viewpoint matches the conclusion reached in chapter two of this work—the signs of the times as delineated in the Olivet Discourse began in Jesus' generation, especially surrounding the events of the fall of Jerusalem in A.D. 70. If that is so, then the preceding four views are rendered untenable, including the perspective that the last generation did not begin until Israel returned to its land in 1948. The upshot of this finding is that it is a mistake to equate the current generation exclusively with the last generation.

Conclusion

We conclude this chapter by reviewing our answers to the questions raised regarding five key eschatological texts appealed to by the doomsday approach. Did Israel's return to its land in 1948 begin the fulfillment of the Abrahamic covenant (Genesis 15:18)? Not necessarily. While we believe the rebirth of Israel this generation may well be providential, it may not be eschatological. That eventuality may continue to elude us for years, and even centuries, to come. Will Russia invade Israel at the end of time (Ezekiel 38—39)? We do not disagree that there will be an invasion of Israel at the end of time. However, there is no solid biblical evidence connecting that invasion with Russia. Will the antichrist rule over a revived Roman Empire (Daniel 2 and 7)? That the antichrist will some day arise and wreak havoc on the earth is a clear teaching in the Bible. But that he will rule a revived Roman Empire is a faulty interpretation of the identification of Daniel's fourth empire. That kingdom was ancient Greece, not the modern European Common Market. Is Daniel's seventieth week imminent (Daniel 9:24-27)? Our exegesis showed that the culprit referred to in Daniel 9:24-27 was Antiochus Epiphanes and that his expulsion from Jerusalem and the subsequent rededication of the temple in 164 B.C. takes one a long way toward the fulfillment of Daniel's seventy weeks or 490 years (though it is not restricted to that time period). Are we living in the last generation (Mark 13:30)? We argued that the generation that would not pass away before the fulfillment of "all these things" referred to in Mark 13:30 was that of *Jesus'* contemporaries, and that "these things" referred to the events attending the fall of Jerusalem in A.D. 70.

If these answers represent accurate interpretations of the five biblical passages discussed in this chapter, what are we to make of the doomsday preachers who point to the current generation as the last generation before the return of Christ? Well, their predictions could come true; all things are possible. But if they do, it will be more so because of luck rather than sound exegesis of the Scriptures, which alone are the Christian's authority.

4

The Separation of the Saints

The Doomsday Mentality & the Danger of Sectarianism

A S WE HAVE SEEN IN THE PREVIOUS CHAPTERS, CERTAIN EVAN-
gelicals, because of their methods of interpretation, believe that the
end of the world began in 1948 when Israel became a modern state
and that we are now living in the final generation before Christ's
return.

Their method of interpretation also leads them to read current
events back into the Bible. They interpret present developments on
the world scene as fulfillments of biblical prophecies. We do not wish
to simply deny that these phenomena are fulfilling Scripture; God may
indeed be working out his plans for the end times even now. We feel,
however, that the doomsday mentality forces people to insist that,
because we are living in the last generation, current events are *necessarily* fulfillments of biblical prophecy.

The doomsday mentality does not emerge in a vacuum. Simply put,
drastic and unpredictable changes in the normal flow of human events

tend to raise the level of expectancy among Christians for the return of Christ, an attitude promoted by prophetic date setters. A number of such factors are present today. There has been an explosion of books, scholarly and popular, evangelical and nonevangelical, commenting on such troubling trends as the continuing deterioration of American society, the worldwide political upheaval that began with the end of the Cold War and the increase in the number of natural disasters.[1] Millennial fever is also being fueled by the fact that we are approaching the end of the second Christian millennium. As the year 2000 looms in the near future, apocalyptic date setters find it easy to connect the end of the millennium with the end of the world. If people believe they are living in the last generation, they think it only logical that God would plan the end of human history within the framework of historical epochs. What better way to bring finality to the world than at the end of a millennium?[2]

Do declines in moral values, increases in global political tension and perceived anomalies in the world of nature, and the end of chronological eras clearly indicate that the Second Coming is at hand? History shows that there have been other eras in which disturbing circumstances existed. Also, as we have seen previously, those waiting for the Second Coming as the year A.D. 1000 approached were greatly disappointed when the new millennium began and Christ did not return. When people believe that the end is upon us, the events in a turbulent world are interpreted in terms of how they fulfill prophecy. We believe that those who embrace the doomsday mentality will be greatly tempted to abandon society, separating themselves from a world that is, in their thinking, on the verge of apocalyptic destruction. Sadly, however, such action undermines Christ's call to be the salt of the earth and the light of the world.

This current phenomenon is not unlike the American modernist-fundamentalist controversy of the 1920s, a time of intense debate between liberal theologians (who had departed from historic Christianity) and fundamentalist theologians (who espoused such basic tenets of Christianity as the necessity of the new birth, the inspiration of the Bible and the deity of Christ). Added to this furor were the signs of societal upheaval that were generated, in part, by World War I and the Great Depression. Gone were the days of the late nineteenth century, when postmillennialism,[3] with its optimistic view of history, dominated, and people generally felt the world was getting better. Also fueling the debate was the rising influence of Darwin's theory of evolution. When the smoke cleared, the fundamentalists found themselves forced out of the mainstream. They responded by withdrawing from society and forming Bible prophecy conferences as rallying points. Generally speaking, these sessions emphasized the erosion of society, and those attending them anxiously awaited the return of Christ to deliver them from the world.[4]

Ironically, as evangelicals withdrew from the mainstream, their influence diminished, and the larger culture only decayed further. This seems similar to what is happening today. By separating from a society that seems to distance itself more from biblical principles with each passing day, some evangelicals have withdrawn the very witness that might contribute to societal reform.

It is interesting to observe the ways in which a given understanding of biblical prophecy affects the interpretation of world events. Let us take as an example Hal Lindsey's recent book, *Planet Earth—2000 A.D.: Will Mankind Survive?* Lindsey, who subscribes to the theory that we are living in the last generation before Christ's return, spends 270 pages of his 312-page book describing all of the troubling phenomena that are occurring today. He discusses the deterioration of moral standards in our society; the movement toward one world religion and government; the increase in UFO sightings; the destruction of the environment; the spread of uncontrollable diseases; the coming crises in worldwide famine and starvation; and the continuing volatile political crisis in the Middle East. All of these things, Lindsey concludes, point to the fact that the end is coming very soon. "I believe we are on the very brink of it [the Rapture]," he says at the end of the book.[5]

Another social observer who believed the Second Coming must be near because of certain contemporary events made similar comments. He wrote that he had become exhausted recording "the daily records of desolating earthquakes, sweeping fires, distressing poverty, natural perplexity, political profligacy, private bankruptcy, and wide-spread immorality, which abound in these last days."[6] These things, he said, obviously indicated the Lord was returning immediately. Interestingly, he wrote these words in 1843. This man, who became weary cataloging all of the numerous signs that pointed to the end of the world, was part of a group that became obsessed with the Second Advent, the Millerites, whom we will discuss later in the chapter. The point we wish to make is that many Christians throughout the history of the church have fervently believed that signs and events in their contemporary setting clearly pointed to the Second Coming. Unfortunately, Christians caught up in the doomsday mentality have rarely sought to learn the lessons of history that would temper their views. In almost any generation, believers could have looked back to the mistakes made by those who preceded them in becoming obsessed with interpreting current events as signs of Christ's coming. Obviously none of these prognosticators has yet been correct.

B. J. Oropeza, in his book *99 Reasons Why No One Knows When Christ Will Return,* does an excellent job of succinctly showing how no one can prove that Christ is coming by analyzing such things as current political events and natural disasters. He deals with such familiar issues as Israel becoming a modern state; the alleged rebuilding of the temple; the recent peace accords between Israel and the Arab nations; the role of the European Economic Community; and attempts to identify the whore of Babylon referred to in the book of Revelation. Oropeza notes that those who make confident statements about the significance of certain events seem to be always changing their minds so that a new scenario may emerge when the old one is proved false. The huge proliferation of literature on the Second Coming during the Persian Gulf War is a good example. Saddam Hussein was reviving the Babylonian Empire, it was thought, and would drag the world into an apocalyptic war. It was the beginning of the end. After the Iraqi army was completely routed in a few days, the prognosticators had to go back to the drawing board. Oropeza also states that such disasters as famine and starvation are very unlikely to occur on a large scale.

Although these are serious issues worthy of our concern and calling for our support for those in need, they only affect about one percent of the world's population. Some claim that an increased number of earthquakes in the twentieth century is a sure sign that Christ is about to come back. Oropeza responds that the scientific data show that there have not been more earthquakes in this century; the technology that is used to detect them has just improved substantially. He also states that more people died in the seventeenth century than in the twentieth as a result of earthquakes.[7] Lastly, one cannot discount the effect that satellite technology has had through such media organizations as CNN, which can now instantly broadcast to the entire world headline-making wars and disasters in any part of the world. Perhaps we feel more crises are occurring because we now have immediate knowledge of all of them.[8]

No one can deny that we are in the midst of extraordinary changes in our society and in the world as a whole. These events, however, can be interpreted and dealt with in a number of ways. Many Christians will adapt to the conditions and find a way to survive and even experience spiritual renewal and vitality in the midst of the anxiety caused by social and political changes. Even now revival is present in several areas of the country and may spread nationwide to transform our moral landscape. Some believers have recently expressed great hope in the future and declared, contrary to the prophets of doom, that the coming years will be a great time of growth and development for evangelicals, whom they call to rise above victimhood and utilize the power of the gospel.[9]

At the end of 1994, *Newsweek* published a special edition which included predictions about what the next century holds for the world. Some issues discussed certainly cause concern: exploding urban populations, the need to protect the environment, the increasingly violent nature of crime. But, for the most part, the special report focused on innovations in such things as transportation, farming, community planning, medicine and global economic markets—innovations which may make our lives much better and the dawn of the new millennium very exciting.[10] But for some evangelicals who believe that we are definitely living in the last generation, societal and global changes are not viewed as opportunities for growth, progress and, especially, ministry, but only as proof that the world is growing more chaotic as the Second Coming approaches. Surely, they reason, all the signs for the Lord's return are being made manifest.

The doomsday mentality, as we will see, leads people to give up on society: If the Lord is returning very soon, why spend time trying to heal the wounds of a dying world? Ironically, evangelicals, the very people who believe they have the ultimate answer to the world's problems, may very likely pull themselves out of the places where that message needs to be proclaimed. How will Christians who take on these beliefs interpret and react to troubling and chaotic conditions in our own culture and around the world? We fear that evangelicals caught in this predicament could begin to exhibit the characteristics of cults by breaking away not only from the threatening secular society but also from the fellowship of other believers, and by adopting heretical beliefs that might lead to dangerous and unbiblical behavior.

How might such a scenario unfold?[11] Those adhering to the dooms-day mentality believe that the world is spiraling out of control and will only continue to get worse because the end is near. Any hope they had for change in the larger culture has been crushed by secularization and new value systems that have gained acceptance and run contrary to biblical standards. They will feel politically powerless to make any significant change in the current cultural Zeitgeist through traditional channels. They will likely interpret current events as fulfillments of biblical prophecy. Further, as evil forces take over the world in preparation for the coming tribulation, a need will arise for "true" Christians, that is, those who know the end is near, to band together and separate themselves from the corruption around them.

Their separation may not end with non-Christians. The Lord's imminent return will be the total focus of their lives, so they may reject fellow evangelicals who do not adopt their views of the end times. In a very short time they may cut themselves off from all outside sources of communication. To keep the remnant together and to protect against undesirable influences, they may insist on complete allegiance to the group and put their faith in a charismatic leader who claims to have been divinely endowed with special gifts. In their obsessive anticipation of the Apocalypse, all other duties and responsibilities will be dropped. This may even apply to theological standards: Eschatology may become the exclusive focus of faith, precluding all other doctrines, which may lead to date setting and other unbiblical practices. The consequences of such behavior can only be destructive.

Historical Illustrations

We might think that it is impossible for evangelicals to do such things. Yet the history of the church is full of examples of dedicated Christians breaking off from the mainstream of society and the rest of Christianity, and becoming obsessed with the Second Coming of Christ. Let us examine a few such examples. As early as the second century A.D., in Phrygia, Asia Minor, a new convert, Montanus, declared that he was the Holy Spirit incarnate who was to reveal what was to come. Montanus and those who flocked to his side experienced visions related to the Second Coming. They said the New Jerusalem would descend on Phrygia, where all Christians were called to come together, repent and await Christ's return. Montanism, which emphasized the renouncing of the world, the necessity of suffering and the exaltation of martyrdom, spread quickly when the Roman Empire revived the persecution of Christians in A.D. 177. The political and social forces of the day, combined with Montanus's charisma and eloquence, attracted so many followers that a new town was created in order to house them all. Montanism was eventually condemned, but its influence was substantial, especially on those overcome with anxiety regarding the events of the day.[12]

Among those who tried to discourage millennial speculations, which were becoming excessive and exaggerated, was the great Augustine of Hippo. He reinterpreted the prophetic passages regarding Christ's Second Coming and claimed that they were meant to be interpreted figuratively, not literally. In his influential work *The City of God,* he wrote that the book of Revelation was meant to be taken as an allegory. For instance, there would be no literal thousand-year millennium. The number one thousand was used only as a metaphor for the extended reign of Christ that began with his birth and was fully realized in the church. Augustine was held in high regard in the church, and his view became the orthodox position after the literal interpretation of the millennium was condemned.[13]

Augustine's interpretation was challenged almost a millennium later by Joachim of Fiore, an Italian monk who lived during the twelfth century. As the leading biblical prophecy scholar of his day, he brought the interpretation of biblical eschatology back to a literal perspective. In his writings on the subject, which he began after he experienced what he called visions of the Apocalypse, the literal interpretation method was taken to extremes. What Joachim added to hermeneutics was the belief that through the correct interpretation of prophecy, one could forecast the course of history. To Joachim, the members of the Godhead represented the three eras in the ascent of history: the Age of the Father (or the law) was characterized by fear; in the Age of the Son (or the gospel), faith reigned; but the Age of the Spirit would be full of love and freedom and the direct revelation of God to his people. Joachim believed his own time to be one of crisis that was about to inaugurate the Age of the Spirit, which would commence with the destruction of the antichrist. Joachim was also a date-setter: he predicted the end would come between 1200 and 1260. The way would be prepared by a new order of monks who would preach the gospel to all nations. Many sought the humble Joachim's insights into deciphering prophecy, including Richard the Lion-Hearted, whom Joachim advised (rather poorly one might add) regarding the Third Crusade, which was considered, like many of the others, a failure. Certain points of Joachim's theology were condemned at the Fourth Lateran Council in 1215, but his influence in reviving the literal interpretation of Scripture regarding the last days was felt for centuries to come in several millenarian movements, and his system reigned until the advent of Marxism.[14] Note that even seven hundred years ago an Italian monk was interpreting the tumultuous events of his own day as signs of the Second Coming and then creating a system to rationalize his beliefs—and perhaps pacify his fears.

Thomas Müntzer and the Peasants' War

One of the most fascinating periods in the history of the church to witness the eruption of millennial expectation was the Reformation. In examining the beliefs and practices of Thomas Müntzer, who paid homage to Joachim, one finds not only the leader of a movement whose core theological foundation was the expectation of the millennium (to be inaugurated through radical social revolution), but also one in whom many modern evangelicals find their spiritual roots.

Luther's movement was still very young when some voices of opposition began claiming reform had not been completed. Those who opposed Luther felt it was not enough for the church to reform; all of society must be transformed, even razed and rebuilt, to achieve biblical standards. Luther, on the other hand, was quite comfortable working with princes whom he perceived to be godly. Members of the nobility even made it possible for him to survive his battles with the Church of Rome by providing shelter and political protection. In Luther's theological matrix, the realms of church and state were separated, leaving political concerns to the powers that be. Secular authority should lie with the nobility, not the masses, who were far too radical and could destroy the entire reform movement with their extreme behavior. The Word of God must be preached and taught—those were Luther's concerns.[15]

Among Luther's most severe critics was Müntzer, known as a remarkably learned intellectual, a theologian well versed in the Bible and the church fathers. Under the influence of Luther, Müntzer turned from Catholic orthodoxy but later broke away from the mainstream Protestant reform movement because of theological differences. Lutherans emphasized the necessity of faith and the foundation of the Bible; Müntzer, a key figure among the Revolutionary Spiritualists, held to a form of mysticism focused on the radical role of the Holy Spirit in the believer's life through personal religious experience. Müntzer's mysticism was wedded to a practical mandate for societal reforms, the most urgent of which regarded the poor treatment of the peasants. Müntzer came to believe that social change may have to take place through armed revolution. Such violent action was driven—and legitimized—by Müntzer's radical views of the Second Coming. In a typical expression of the doomsday mentality, Müntzer even claimed that Luther, because of his conservative social views, was the beast referred to in Revelation. Müntzer was renounced by the Lutherans; one biography of him, whose authorship has been attributed to Philipp Melanchthon, claimed he was a fanatic, even demon-possessed. By 1524, Müntzer's views had propelled him into leading what has become known as the Peasants' War, which was to claim more than a hundred thousand lives, including his own.[16]

Over the years that led up to that point, Müntzer's views became progressively more unorthodox. His commitment to social revolution as a means of ushering in the millennium was solidified as he became exposed to such radical thinkers as Nicholas Storch, a leader of the Zwickau prophets, who resuscitated the beliefs of the Taborites, a fifteenth-century millenarian group. Storch was so opposed to the established order that he called for the armed revolt of the "elect" to destroy the ungodly, which he believed would usher in the millennium. Müntzer accepted Storch's views and taught that the true believer must prepare himself for this apocalyptic battle by renouncing all physical pleasure and embracing personal suffering. The peasants were identified as the elect because they were the ones best prepared to understand and face this challenge.[17]

Müntzer's views soon became politicized and greatly influenced the way in which he interpreted the events of the day. In the summer of 1524 a series of peasant revolts broke out, and Müntzer believed that his prophecies were being fulfilled. Interestingly, many of the rebels were not from the lowest and most oppressed classes, but were those who felt the frustration of barriers that prohibited their further social and economic growth. Müntzer became the intellectual leader of this peasants' revolt. Through his millenarianism, the peasants found a spiritual foundation for their violent rebellion. They also found that they were elevated to the heights of the elect; they now saw themselves as an exclusive group, specially chosen by God. Müntzer interpreted the uprisings as the collapse of the fifth monarchy prophesied in the book of Daniel, which he himself foretold in his famous

Sermon Before the Princes. He also believed he was a great warrior (he bestowed upon himself military titles, such as "Thomas Müntzer with the sword of Gideon") who would lead the peasants into the millennium.[18]

The peasants, however, were no match for the imperial military forces that were called in to suppress the rebellion. On May 14, 1525, Müntzer led a band of his followers into a one-sided battle in which four thousand peasants died. Müntzer himself escaped but was later captured, tortured, forced to sign a recantation of his views and then beheaded. The plight of the peasants only worsened after the rebellions ceased; the nobility and ecclesiastical authorities grew even stronger and were determined to suppress the masses even further to keep them in line.[19]

Müntzer's ideals did not die with him. For example, some Anabaptists, who considered Müntzer a spiritual patriarch for their movement, followed his revolutionary method of forcing change on society to correct its ills. One particular group under the leadership of Jan Matthys took control of the city of Münster in 1534. They asserted it was the New Jerusalem, condemned to death all whom they considered ungodly and claimed that Christ would return soon. The so-called New Jerusalem, however, eventually became a killing field. After laying siege to the city for months (and after several dates predicting the Second Coming came and went), government soldiers slaughtered the Anabaptists in a surprise attack in June 1535. For years, the Anabaptists, who for the most part practiced pacifism, would be despised for what happened at Münster.[20]

Unfortunately, this was a large part of Thomas Müntzer's legacy. One finds it hard to imagine how someone who had begun with orthodox convictions and motivations and a desire to help the poor and disenfranchised could end his life so violently because of a distorted eschatology, an eschatology which drove him increasingly further from the gospel he sought to proclaim. He justified the violence he encouraged through the pretense that it would usher in the millennium. Müntzer's vision became his own apocalyptic nightmare. It is even more tragic that his actions were repeated by his followers.

In other respects, however, when one observes the progression of Müntzer's behavior, one finds that his demise was unavoidable. Müntzer became disenchanted when his calls for further reform were not accepted by Luther and his followers. Müntzer isolated himself from his fellow believers and adopted radical millennial views which influenced all of his thinking. He created a system in which only the "elect," that is, those who adopted his beliefs, especially the peasants, would enter into the millennium. The elect, then, were an exclusive group, the true remnant, set in opposition to all other members of society.

As Müntzer became fixated on the Second Coming, everything else became secondary and was interpreted through that matrix. So, it was quite natural for him to read such political events of his day as the Peasants' Revolt in terms of their fulfilling biblical prophecy. Müntzer did not set specific dates for the Second Coming, but he firmly believed that the great event was about to happen and that he was God's choice for ushering in the millennium.

With these highly charged views, Müntzer became an inspirational leader of the peasants, who found in him an explanation for their struggle and vindication for their violent actions. In return, Müntzer demanded total commitment from his elect—no one could stray from the ultimate goal of inaugurating the millennium. Their protests against their socioeconomic hardships were seen in a new and powerful light: they were the the chosen ones fighting the oppressive forces of evil. The day had arrived for them to crush God's enemies; those without pedigree would now finally enjoy political power.

Many of Müntzer's disciples charged into battle and died believing they were fulfilling God's will. It is remarkable how the great hope of Christ's coming can be used to justify any number of causes and theories gone awry. In the end, one must remember that becoming obsessed with interpretations regarding the millennium has real and often bitter consequences.

We might observe Müntzer and the Anabaptists and conclude that because this happened so long ago and because their behavior was so bizarre, evangelicals simply could not get caught up in such things today. To show that it could happen in our own time, we would like to jump forward from sixteenth-century Europe to a movement in America that reached its peak just 150 years ago and that was also obsessed with predictions the Second Coming. Thousands of its followers became disillusioned with Christianity or adopted heretical beliefs when the predictions did not come to pass.

The Millerites
"I was thus brought, in 1818, at the close of my two years' study of the Scriptures, to the solemn conclusion, that in about twenty-five years from that time all the affairs of our present state would be wound up." In this nonchalant and unassuming manner William Miller, a self-educated New York farmer and newly converted Baptist, predicted that the return of Christ would occur "about the year 1843" and gave birth to a mass movement that swept the United States, convincing tens of thousands of people that the world was about to end.[21]

What makes Millerism so important to our discussion is that the profile of the Millerites and their experiences parallel that of today's evangelicals. We may look to them as perhaps the most precise example in the history of Christianity of what could happen to evangelicals who accept unquestioningly the idea that 1948 marked the beginning of the end and that the year 2000 is a benchmark by which the last days should be calculated. When one discusses groups who respond to the expectation of the millennium with cultlike behavior, one thinks of those on the fringes of society. One may even interpret the Peasants' War in such a way—Müntzer merely led a body of disenfranchised peasants astray. Surely the same could never happen to the average evangelical today. But what most Millerites had in common was that the great majority were average, middle-class evangelical Christians, orthodox in their beliefs and enjoying comfortable positions in society.

Yet, these mainstream, rational people eventually became obsessed with the imminence of the Second Advent and withdrew from society, forming a separatist sect. Once they cut themselves off from the mainstream of society and from ties to their local churches, they set themselves up for disaster. We will deal with the results and fallout of their behavior in the next chapter. Here, we wish to discuss what led William Miller's followers to become intensely preoccupied with the coming of the millennium and to break away and separate themselves from the orthodox moorings of their local churches to pursue what they considered a purer form of Christianity. All of this did not happen instantaneously; one may trace the sequence of events that led many, who at one time had been strong evangelical Christians, to eventually renounce their faith or adopt heretical beliefs and practices.

William Miller was born on February 15, 1782, in Pittsfield, Massachusetts. His formal educational experience was limited, but he had a voracious love of books and learning. He married and settled in Low Hampton, New York, where he had been raised, and became a farmer. Miller was a deist, having rejected most of the Christian beliefs he was taught by his pious Christian mother. In 1816, however, Miller fell under sustained spiritual conviction and converted to Christianity. After a two-year study, using only a Bible and a concordance, he came to a dramatic and extraordinary conclusion: Christ would return very soon, probably about 1843.[22]

Miller's theory was quite elaborate, but central to it was his interpretation of two verses in the book of Daniel which he tied together to supply the elements necessary to calculate the Lord's return: Daniel 8:14, "And he said to me, Unto two thousand and three hundred days; then shall the sanctuary be cleansed" (KJV) and 9:24, "Seventy weeks were determined upon thy people and upon thy holy city, to finish the transgression, and to make an end of sins, and to make a reconciliation for iniquity, and to bring in everlasting righteousness, and to seal up the vision and prophecy, and to anoint the most Holy" (KJV). Miller's basic reasoning can be outlined as follows:

1. The sanctuary cleansing mentioned in Daniel 8:14 referred to the return of Christ which would eradicate all evil on the earth.

2. A prophetic day equaled one year, so one could correctly calculate the numbers in the passages as 2,300 years and 490 years (70 times 7).

3. Using Bishop Ussher's popular Old Testament chronology, the 2,300-year period began with the return of the Jews to Jerusalem to rebuild the city in 457 B.C. (Christ's crucifixion, A.D. 33, marked the

end of Daniel's seventy weeks; moving back 490 years from A.D. 33, one comes to the year 457 B.C.).

4. 2,300 years forward from 457 B.C. was A.D. 1843.[23]

Miller kept his discovery secret, fearing he would mislead people if he were wrong. He spent five more years rechecking the passages and his figures. In 1831, with great reluctance, he made his findings public.[24]

Miller's theory, the delivery of which he considered a lecture, not a sermon, was instantly accepted. The church where he first presented it in a Sunday morning service invited him back to speak throughout the week. Revival spread quickly through that church soon after Miller's presentation. He became a popular speaker and had to turn down more invitations than he could accept. In 1833, he was issued a license to preach by his Baptist church, and he published a pamphlet outlining his beliefs.[25] Three years later he published his first book, *Evidences from Scripture and History of the Second Coming of Christ About the Year 1843: Exhibited in a Course of Lectures.* Miller spoke to large crowds, many of whom included significant numbers of clergymen from various denominations. By 1838, he was delivering two lectures a day. His audiences, however, were mostly found in small New England towns. He had never spoken in a major city, nor would he lecture without an invitation. This changed when Miller met Joshua V. Himes.[26]

The proclamation of Miller's message exploded in 1840 when Himes, pastor of the Chardon Street Chapel in Boston, joined Miller to become his promoter. Himes quickly began incorporating various public relations techniques to reach a mass audience. He booked Miller and aspiring Millerite itinerant speakers in large metropolitan halls instead of waiting to be invited to rural churches. Miller's message spread even more quickly through several publishing endeavors Himes developed. He founded a number of newspapers in major American metropolitan cities, including the *Signs of the Times* (Boston), the *Midnight Cry* (New York) and the *Philadelphia Alarm,* which expounded Miller's views and answered his growing number of critics. Himes formed a network of salesmen who distributed an assortment of books, tracts and other Millerite literature. He also published popular charts, visually depicting Miller's calculations, and even compiled a book of hymns, *The Millennial Harp,* with adventist themes. Himes's expertise in publicity and organization provided the means by which Miller's views were transported from rural New England to a national audience.[27]

One technique Himes employed more than any other, the camp meeting, brought Millerism to untold thousands of people. The denominations had used these revival gatherings in rural locations to take the faith to the frontier where churches had not yet been founded. Himes proved to be a master at managing these events in order to reach large numbers quickly. Millerite leaders focused on the mass appeal of camp meetings because by the summer of 1842 they were consumed with the urgency of their mission—their leader was teaching that Christ would probably return in a year. The intensity of their effort is sensed in this letter published in the *Signs of the Times:*

> But with so short a time to awake the slumbering virgins, and save souls, we must *work; work* night and day. God has thrust us out in haste, to give the *last* invitation, and we must labor in earnest, and *compel* them to come in, that His house may be filled. . . . The midnight cry must yet be made to ring, and ring through every valley and over every hilltop and plain. . . . They must be made to feel that it is *now or never.* And they will.[28]

The camp meetings were immediately successful. The first official one, held in June 1842 at East Kingston, New Hampshire, reached an estimated ten to fifteen thousand people over an eight-day period. With donations contributed at that first camp meeting, a fifty-foot high tent (one of the largest of its day) to seat three to four thousand people was commissioned to be built. The Millerites now had their own mobile hall. By the end of 1842, thirty camp meetings had been held in just four months, the Great Tent being transported with speed and efficiency from city to city.[29]

Through 1842 Miller had predicted that Christ would return "about" 1843. At the beginning of 1843, Miller specifically calculated (or perhaps recalculated) the Second Advent to occur between March

21, 1843, and March 21, 1844. To some it may have seemed as if Miller were hedging his bets, allowing a wider time span for the Lord's return than he had originally proposed. Yet, Millerism's popularity only increased. For example, in February 1843, Miller rented the Chinese Museum, a large hall in Philadelphia, for thirteen days. The attendance for one meeting alone was estimated by a secular newspaper at between four and five thousand.[30]

By early 1843 the movement had become so extensive that the Millerites had to build their own meeting place in Boston, an auditorium that could seat thirty-five hundred, because there was no other building that could hold them all. The spread of the Millerite movement reached northeast throughout New England, north to Canada, south to Virginia and Kentucky, and west to Ohio. Millerite newspapers even received letters from Indiana, Illinois and Wisconsin—then considered the Western frontier. At the end of 1843, Miller called for the distribution of one million tracts.[31] By January 1844, Miller claimed he had delivered "4,500 lectures in about 12 years to at least 500,000 different people."[32] It has been estimated that at the height of the movement's popularity, Miller could boast between thirty thousand and one-hundred thousand followers.[33]

The Coming Separation
Ironically, in the midst of incredible growth and popularity, Millerism was slowly becoming a separatist movement, which eventually led to catastrophic ends. We will set the stage for discussing why that happened by exploring four areas: (1) the profile of those joining the movement, (2) the movement's conservative nature and theological tenets, (3) the way in which Millerites were interpreting the events of the day and (4) the unstable social and cultural context of the time. Note the parallels to our own day.

1. Millerism not only attracted people from the mainstream of society, it was a mass movement, reaching tens of thousands of people, not a mere handful of believers as is typical of most cultlike millenarian movements. In studies that have been conducted, one finds that the great majority of Millerites were gainfully employed: some were

farmers, businessmen or industrialists; others were craftsmen, laborers, clerks or professionals. Interestingly, a significant number of Millerites were clergymen from orthodox evangelical churches. Nearly two-thirds of the Millerites came from Methodist or Baptist churches; the rest had Congregational, Christian or Presbyterian denominational ties.[34] At that time most of these churches held to evangelical doctrinal positions.

2. At the beginning of the movement, Millerism's theological tenets could easily be accepted by most evangelicals. At conferences convened by Millerites to clarify their beliefs, their stated doctrinal positions, except for the 1843 prediction, were particularly orthodox. Miller considered himself a Calvinist Baptist. He disliked any overt appeals to emotion, refusing to use such popular revivalist techniques as the "anxious bench" (a place near the front of an auditorium or church where those who responded to an altar call went to pray about their need for salvation). As the movement grew in popularity, he was adamant that his followers not start a new sect but stay in their respective churches, fearing a tide of extremism, which he greatly opposed.[35] In defending himself against criticism, Miller tried to state clearly where he stood: "I have not countenanced fanaticism in any form. I use no dreams or visions except those in the Word of God. I have not advised anyone to separate from the churches to which they may have belonged, unless their brethren cast them out or deny them religious privileges. I have taught you no precept of man; nor the creed of any sect. I have never designed to make a new sect."[36] The report of the first Millerite conference in October 1840 reflects the founder's sentiments: "We are not of those who sow discord among brethren, who withdraw from the fellowship of the churches, who rail at the office of the ministry, and triumph in the exposure of the errors of a secular and apostate church, and who count themselves holier than others, or wiser than their fellows."[37]

Not only did Miller want his followers to stay in their churches, but records show that Methodist and Baptist churches reached attendance peaks in New England during the time when Millerism had its greatest influence there. Churches in other areas, where the movement was not as effective, did not experience the same growth. Millerism was obviously a positive influence in getting people into Protestant churches.[38] Interestingly, the region where this church growth occurred included the "Burned-over District," an area in New York State that had experienced so much revival and the advent of alternative Christian sects that the people there were considered "burned out" on Christianity.[39]

Even at the beginning of 1843, the predicted year of the Second Advent, Miller warned his followers not to abandon their normal lives because of Christ's imminent return:

> To conclude that we have nothing to do by way of laboring for the souls of others or providing for our temporal wants, and therefore spend our time in idleness, is to disobey God and bring dishonor on the cause we have espoused. . . . Let [everyone] continue to sow his field and gather the fruits of the earth while seedtime and harvest may continue, neglecting none of the duties of this life.[40]

Lastly, Miller did not bear any of the obvious signs of a cultlike leader. Such figures are usually megalomaniacs, having charismatic personalities and a hunger for power that demands total allegiance to their will. Miller has been described as thoroughly lacking charm and magnetism. He allowed leaders within his movement to disagree with its central tenet: the return of Christ by March 1844.[41] One *New York Herald* reporter covering a camp meeting described Miller in this way:

> In person he is about five feet seven inches in height, very thick set, broad shoulders; lightish brown hair, a little bald, a benevolent countenance, full of wrinkles, and his head shakes as though he was slightly afflicted with the palsy. His manners are very much in his favor; he is not a very well-educated man; but he has read and studied history and prophecy very closely; has much strong common sense, and is evidently sincere in his belief.[42]

Millerite doctrines were orthodox, and Miller himself sought neither to form his own sect nor to engage in any behavior that was in the least bit peculiar. The only difference between Millerites and their evangelical brethren was in their eschatological beliefs. Millerites held that the Second Coming would occur by 1844, and they embraced premil-

lennialism against the predominant postmillennialism of the day.
3. The Millerites were orthodox evangelicals, the vast majority
of whom seem to have been normal people. They were encouraged
by the movement's leadership to stay in their churches. What led
them to separate from the larger evangelical world and form their
own sect? Michael Barkun is particularly helpful in exploring this
question in that he examines the manner in which Millerites interpreted current events and the social and cultural context in which
they lived. He notes that Millerite literature is full of searches for
fulfillments of biblical prophecy in the day's political crises and
natural disasters. These events were divine signs that the Second
Advent was approaching. Miller himself would read the prophetic
biblical text and then try to find its consummation in what was
occurring at the time. Unrest and revolution were sure signs of the
Lord's return. In 1840 Josiah Litch, a prominent Millerite leader,
predicted that on August 11 of that year a great world war would
break out in the Middle East over the Ottoman Empire. He said he
found the war prophesied in the book of Revelation. When that date
came and went without incident, Litch published a response: "I am
entirely satisfied that on the 11th of August, 1840, *the Ottoman
power according to previous calculation,* DEPARTED TO RE-
TURN NO MORE. I can now say with the utmost confidence, 'the
second woe is past and behold the third woe cometh quickly.'"[43]
Such strategies employed to deal with unfulfilled Millerite prophecies would later lead to dire consequences for the movement.

Later, other Millerites said that the Catholic and Protestant nations
of Europe would face off in battle. The conflict never materialized.
Ironically, as the Millerites were looking for political upheaval to
confirm their beliefs, the world remained at peace. Of course, the
Millerites interpreted the the international climate of order that pervaded 1843 as merely a facade that covered imminent warfare. Warnings about the outbreak of a world war pervaded the Millerite press.
Domestically, the Millerites decried the deterioration in morals among
Americans and especially warned against the adverse effects of Roman Catholics immigrating into the United States. Not only was it

feared they would destroy Protestant America with their overpowering numbers, but the pope was seen by many Protestants of the time as the antichrist.[44]

The Millerites were overwhelmed to find all manner of unusual phenomena occurring in the world. Natural disasters were just as important as political events because of their inclusion in biblical prophecies as signs of the end times, as this previously cited excerpt from the *Midnight Cry* indicates: "The pen grows weary in recording—and the press in publishing the daily records of desolating earthquakes, sweeping fires, distressing poverty, natural perplexity political profligacy, private bankruptcy, and wide-spread immorality, which abound in these last days."[45]

The Millerites were interpreting these events through the matrix of millennial expectancy. Most of their contemporaries did not find the same significance in these events. Abolitionist William Lloyd Garrison, who knew several Millerite leaders because they were also part of the antislavery movement, noted the following:

It is amusing to see how the most ordinary events are cited by the advocates of this new theory [Millerism], as proofs that "the day of the Lord is at hand." The fire at Hamburgh—the earthquake at Cape Haitien—falling of the chandelier in the U.S. House of Representatives—the pecuniary embarrassments of the times—these, and many other equally *remarkable* occurrences, are set forth as solemn warnings.[46]

4. A series of crises in New York State, the hub of Millerite activity, which began in 1810 and lasted until the middle of the century, may have led some to find the cataclysmic nature of Miller's premillennialism appealing. The worse things got, the more obvious it became that the end might indeed be near. Between 1810 and 1832 a series of floods, epidemics and crop failures plagued the northeastern United States. In a largely agrarian society, many buckled under the stress caused by these events.[47] Following these natural disasters, a national economic crisis which extended from 1837 to 1844 sent many into financial panic, and some were ruined. A banking crisis loomed over the entire area as many financial institutions, overly optimistic about

the economic growth which had begun in the late eighteenth century, had extended credit too far. Family farms were increasingly affected by the national economy because subsistence farming had disappeared. Farmers, who at one time could weather economic hardship because they were producing crops for themselves and their neighbors, were now raising crops for markets that were far away. Suddenly, average farmers were dependent on the larger economy. They needed others to provide what they no longer produced for themselves.[48]

Great fear arose among the people who had to face these circumstances because the traditional agricultural way of life could not be maintained. Population growth, the reorientation of market demands and the growth of commerce and industry all contributed to this change. With the swift growth of the population, affordable farmland was difficult to come by. Continuity in family tradition was greatly disturbed as male children were not able to start their own farms when they came of age, forcing them to venture off to mill and factory towns or head west to the frontier. The once large, stable, extended farm family was now breaking up because of uncontrollable economic forces.[49]

These events may have left many with the feeling that things could not get worse and that, indeed, the world was about to end. Further, although these events did not touch the lives of most Millerites directly, one may assume that the entire New England area felt a shocking sense of anxiety as the basic societal structure in a part of the region broke down in a short period of time. One may see the parallels with our present circumstances. Such things as the breakdown of the family and moral values, the perceived influence of and persecution by anti-Christian forces, worldwide political upheaval, natural disasters and uncontrollable diseases have created an air of instability and chaos in foundational areas of society and have contributed to the conviction among many that Christ must return soon.

In summary, the Millerites were a group of rational, middle-class and very orthodox evangelicals who seem to have become caught up in millennial expectation which influenced the way they interpreted the political events and natural phenomena of the time. Many of them may also have been anticipating the Second Advent because of societal and financial crises that were affecting the region. These factors are important in understanding what happened to the movement.

The Separation Begins

In 1843, as Millerism grew in popularity, the distinctives between the movement and the established denominations became more pronounced. Many clergymen felt that Millerism's overemphasis on the imminent return of Christ left no room for any other manifestation of the faith. They also criticized Miller's interpretation of the biblical texts and chastised him for at least seeming to set a date for the Second Coming, something the Bible clearly states that no one knows (Mt 24:36). Other clergymen were jealous of Millerism's popularity. There was more attention paid to the movement than to the local churches. If they were not envious of the attention Millerism was receiving, they were frightened by the sheer size of the movement—tens of thousands were becoming Millerites. With the fear and jealousy came sharp-edged responses, both legitimate and mean-spirited, to Millerism.[50]

On the other hand, some Millerites felt spiritually suppressed because they were not free to express themselves in their churches. Millerites were renewed and reawakened in the movement's meetings, making their faith exciting. Because of the urgency of the movement's message, Millerites became aggressive and, some felt, self-righteous and obnoxious in asserting their views regarding the Second Advent. Their bold proclamations were not met with enthusiasm in local churches, which now seemed cold and lifeless to them. As Millerites grew more committed to the imminent Second Advent, many denominational churches grew more distant and wary of the movement. The desire among many Millerites for separation only became stronger as time passed.[51] Millerites had become obsessed with the coming of the Second Advent, looking for signs in current events. Because of the social and economic upheaval in the region, they became even more fixated on the Lord's return. The pursuit of the great event was their all-consuming passion. Many people left behind commitments they had made and focused exclusively on the Lord's return. For example, several Millerite leaders, most notably Miller himself and Himes, were vocal abolitionists, but once the movement took shape they abandoned the antislavery cause. Suddenly, everything paled and lacked significance in light of the Second Advent. Given this, it is not difficult to understand why they separated from their Christian brethren.[52]

Separation began to be discussed in the Millerite press. One of the movement's leaders, Silas Hawley, noted in the *Midnight Cry* that new converts who did not get involved in a local denominational church seemed to be thriving in the faith, while those who joined churches "are dying in religion, and are giving up the doctrine of the speedy appearing. They have spiritual asthma; it is hard for them to breathe."[53]

It was prominent Millerite leader Charles Fitch, however, who sounded the battle cry that would resound throughout the ranks of Millerism as a call for sectarian separation: "Come out of her, My people." In the summer of 1843, Fitch preached a sermon by this title, later reprinted in the *Midnight Cry,* taken from Revelation 18:4: "Babylon the great is fallen. Come out of her, My people, that ye be not partakers of her sins, and that ye receive not of her plagues" (KJV). Traditionally, in certain Protestant circles Babylon was thought to refer to the Roman Catholic Church. Fitch reinterpreted the reference to include "Protestant Christendom" also: Protestants as well as Catholics had abandoned the true spirituality of the pure faith. The indifferent, hostile or cold manner in which the Protestant churches were responding to the Millerite declaration of the imminent Second Advent indicated that they had no heart for Christ's return. Fitch pleaded with the Millerites:

To come out of Babylon, is to be converted to the true Scriptural doctrine of the personal coming and kingdom of Christ; . . .

If you are a Christian, *come out of Babylon.* If you intend to be found a Christian when Christ appears, *come out of Babylon,* and come out *now.* Throw away that miserable medley of ridiculous spiritualizing nonsense, with which multitudes have so long been making the Word of God of none effect, and dare to believe the Bible."[54]

Even though many Millerite leaders openly challenged Fitch's interpretation and proposal, many separatists on the grassroots level now had a biblical mandate for withdrawal.

Attacks against the movement did not originate from religious sources alone. The secular press began covering Millerism when it started gaining popularity and public attention. The press had a heyday mocking Millerite camp meetings, rallies and especially the central teaching of the movement that the world was about to end. The press's relentless and biased scrutiny was intensified when Millerism began penetrating major urban centers. The papers were full of exaggerated stories and mocking cartoons and broadsides lambasting the Millerites. In November 1842, as part of a circulation war between the *New York Herald* and the *New York Tribune,* the *Herald* ran a sensationalized ten-part series on the Millerite camp meetings in Newark, New Jersey. Circulation increased when the Millerite stories were published, so the paper made the movement a regular part of its coverage for two years. Ironically, those stories were read by people who were attracted to Millerism as well as by those who found it ridiculous. Himes sent the *Herald* a note thanking them for the coverage, perhaps because the Newark meetings attracted six thousand people.[55]

We noted that religious hostility toward Millerism intensified as the movement grew. As Miller's deadline for the Second Advent (March 21, 1844) neared, people joined the movement at an accelerated pace. Conversely, opposition sharpened. Millerism was no longer just an interchurch movement; it was becoming a powerful force whose members were increasingly aggressive in insisting that the mainline churches listen to their message. As a result, the Millerite press records case after case in which clergy and laypeople were expelled from their churches. Many others left voluntarily.[56]

The lines had been drawn for many Millerites. The editor of the *Midnight Cry,* who had recently chastised Fitch for his interpretation of the Revelation passage, "Come out of her, My people," in February 1844 used those same words in an editorial calling Millerites to withdraw from their hostile churches. One may find a definitive point of separation in the phenomenon that began to emerge at the beginning of 1844. In several locations, Millerites who withdrew or were expelled from their local churches began building Millerite tabernacles (small meeting places) so that they could worship together.[57]

A split began to emerge within the movement itself. Miller, Himes and other members of the movement's leadership promoted toleration and harmony regarding their relationship with the denominations. They rejected any notion of separation, fearing that such a move would take the focus off the Second Advent. Miller even warned that separation could be a tool of Satan for diverting the attention of Millerites. Further, Miller was not sure that he agreed with others in the movement that the pronoun *her* in the Revelation 18:4 passage included to Protestantism.[58]

Great expectation arose as March 21, 1844, approached. Millerites became more vigilant in spreading the message of Christ's return. Unfortunately for them, Christ did not return by March 21. This, of course, ignited a new round of heated criticism from the denominations and lampooning from the scoffing press and general public. Miller's failed prediction became known as the First Disappointment.

One would think that most Millerites would become disillusioned and leave the movement, forced to admit that their critics had been right. But very few, mainly those on the fringes of the movement, left. Most Millerites not only retained their convictions, but, amazingly, they also intensified their efforts to proclaim that the Second Coming was now more imminent than ever. The differences that had split Millerites were put behind them; the First Disappointment created a united front within the movement. Perhaps even more amazingly, as more meetings were held, more new converts entered the fold than ever before. The Millerites were exhibiting a phenomenon which will be discussed in detail in the next chapter. For our purposes here, we must note that the criticism generated by the First Disappointment only solidified the Millerites' move toward sectarian separation. More than ever the Millerites stood alone against the rest of the world.[59] The most obvious manifestation of this occurred just after the First Disappointment. A Millerite newspaper editor suggested that the Millerites change their name to Adventists, which, he said, "marks the real ground of difference between us and the great body of our opponents." (This statement appeared in the newly named *Advent Herald,* formerly the *Signs of the Times.*) The editorial stated that differences between the Millerites and their critics were fixed not only on Miller's date setting, but on the very nature of biblical prophecy.[60]

The separation was made complete when in August 1844 Himes, one of the moderate Millerite leaders who had endorsed unity with the denominations, began to advocate separation. If churches refused to preach the imminent coming of Christ, they must be associated with Babylon. Miller himself did not endorse this view but chose not to oppose it openly this time. In a letter Himes wrote the following:

> We are agreed in the *instant* and final separation from all who oppose the doctrine of the coming and kingdom of God at hand. We believe it to be a case of life and death. It is death to remain connected with those bodies that speak lightly of, or oppose the coming of the Lord. It is life to come out from all human tradition, and stand upon the Word of God, and look daily for the appearing of the Lord. We therefore now say to all who are in any way entangled in the yoke of bondage, "Come out from among them, and be ye *separate,* saith the Lord."[61]

From this point on, the only thing of any importance to the Millerites was the Second Advent. All else was put aside for the sake of their interpretation of this doctrine, with which most of evangelical Christianity did not agree. Fellow Christians were no longer brothers and sisters, but were those who allied themselves with the evils of Babylon, which Fitch identified as "Antichrist," that is, "everything that rises in opposition to the personal reign of Christ on David's throne."[62] The Millerites, now Adventists, "stood sharp and clear on the religious horizon as a well-defined and more or less separate movement, with ministers, Second Advent associations, and meeting houses."[63]

Distracted by the unexpected new life breathed into the movement by the failure of Miller's prediction, the Adventists were not prepared for the coming second disappointment that would destroy their movement. By the end of the year, Millerism would be in disarray, leaving most of its members either severely disillusioned with their faith or adopting heretical beliefs to distract them from the reality they could not face.

Perspective on Sectarian Separation

In the next chapter we will continue the story of the Millerites. Here we want to look at the dynamics of Millerism, which began as an interdenominational movement and ended with its followers left in despair and denial. It is fascinating to note the effect an uneducated lay preacher had on people—because of his rather crude and unsophisticated predictions, thousands became obsessed with the Second Coming. Ironically, by the end, Millerism had become what it had long sought to avoid becoming—a separatist sect that had cut itself off from the fellowship of believers as well as from the secular world.

The social sciences may give us some insight into what happened to the Millerites. In a classic work by sociologist Yonina Talmon,[64] we may not have all the elements for a precise analysis of Millerism, but we do find some common themes in the movement and her discussion of millenarianism. We will use selected parts of her model as a framework for our observations.

Talmon states that millenarianism arises among deprived groups, especially those experiencing unusually harsh suffering and persecution. Interestingly, obsession with the Second Coming is often preceded by natural disasters. This deprivation is usually accompanied by an inability of people to achieve long-held expectations. Millenarian movements may be born in the midst of cultural change and shifts that leave a chasm between what was hoped to be accomplished and the reality that that goal will not come to pass. The chasm that separates the expectation and the reality is joined by the hope of the Second Coming. The Millerites were not only persecuted by fellow Christians and the secular world alike as their movement grew more exclusive, they in all likelihood felt the repercussions of the financial crisis and natural disasters that struck at that time. They did not emerge from the lower, deprived classes, but they did very likely feel a high degree of anxiety and discouragement in the situations they faced.[65]

Millenarian activity also takes place, Talmon asserts, when a new system of values, which runs contrary to prevailing and accepted traditional norms, is introduced into the culture without any means of regulating it. The new system may have greater influence than the traditional one, thus threatening the foundations of the old order, which is questioned as a valid means of representing the culture. Millenarian activity may be prompted by a crusade to recover the sense of what was normal, traditional and right in the eyes of those who feel their culture has crumbled around them. The sense of anxiety produced by such circumstances becomes overwhelming. As Talmon comments, "Millenarianism is often born out of the search for a tolerably coherent system of values, a new cultural identity and regained sense of dignity and self-respect."[66] The Millerites found themselves in the midst of what they considered a highly immoral society in turmoil, racing down a destructive path. Also, the financial and natural crises of the period led, for a significant number, to the disintegration of the family structure as it had been known for generations. Christ must be coming back, they reasoned, because the whole world seems to be falling apart.

Finally, Talmon finds that the loss of the influence of traditional value systems may lead those caught up in millenarian activity to isolate themselves from the larger society. People who feel they are living in a world which has lost its moorings and has turned away from what is right—and even God-ordained—find no place of comfort or peace in the brave new world, so they withdraw from it.[67] The Millerites at first felt the sting of persecution from the mocking secular world. Criticism even came from fellow believers. Eventually, they came to believe that the Christian community had rejected Christ by rejecting the Millerite view of the Second Coming. Millerites also felt a special bond among themselves that they did not experience in their local churches. Acceptance, however, turned to exclusivity and promoted an unhealthy isolationism. The more they separated from fellow believers, the more they adopted unorthodox interpretations of Scripture. "Come out of her, My people," which became the cry of the movement, effectively made fellow Christians the pawns of Satan's schemes. Millerites came to view believers outside the movement as apostates who would be judged along with the unsaved. The Millerites saw themselves as the true remnant, as strangers living in an alien world that did not share their values and which must be abandoned.

Conclusion

A few things stand out in understanding how Millerism became a separate and self-destructive movement. As Talmon notes, prevailing unstable and threatening societal and global conditions and perceived persecution tend to create an atmosphere in which prognosticators start predicting the Second Coming. People ask how things can get any worse and conclude that the Lord must be coming back. Note the explosion in the last thirty years of popular-level prophecy literature during times of distress: the Six Day War in the sixties; the energy crisis and the overthrow of the Shah of Iran by the Ayatollah Khomeini in the seventies; the Cold War showdown during the eighties; the Persian Gulf War in the early nineties; and the continuing decline of family values and the perceived threat of such things as political correctness and multiculturalism. In difficult times the seeds of the doomsday mentality are planted.

Political pundit Charles Krauthammer has written about the adverse effects of the doomsday mentality on the political process and society at large. In one article about the Millerites and their contemporaries in today's society, he concludes his thoughts in the following manner:

Nevertheless, the fact that new Millerites rise and fall every few years doesn't prove that today's Millerites may not in fact be right. Does that mean that we are in an emergency? Yes, but no more than other civilizations, since all are susceptible to destruction. That possibility exists, always, everywhere. Numberless societies have been destroyed by natural disaster, war, and internal collapse. There is a certain hubris in believing that ours is the first to face the prospect. But more than hubris, danger too. Not from the true millennialists, who are passively, and joyously, making their devotions and stocking up on biscuits and distilled water. But from the fretful apocalypticists, whose declarations of emergency—of an ever-changing succession of emergencies—make political claims on all of us. Sidney Hook once said that those who make survival the supreme value are declaring that there is nothing they will not betray. The same holds for those who use the threat of apocalypse as an instrument of political blackmail. That is reason enough to resist the sirens calling us to the moral equivalent of war, and go on with our daily business.[68]

When one predicts that the Lord must return by a certain time, especially when that time is not too far in the future, one unleashes a plethora of unbiblical actions that may have severe consequences. Those who adhere to the prediction begin interpreting everything that happens around them as fulfillments of biblical prophecies that point to the Second Coming. Ironically, instead of creating a state of calm and peace that the imminence of the great event should bring, the doomsday mentality creates an air of anxiety and paranoia on the one hand and surrender and futility regarding the Christian's duty to society on the other hand. The Millerites were no exception to this, interpreting current events and natural disasters as signs of the end.

If one is sure the Lord is definitely returning shortly, the expectation becomes excessive and all-consuming. Everything else in one's life is put aside. The Millerites abandoned the abolitionist movement when they were convinced Christ was returning soon. Why fight for abolition? The slaves will be freed anyway, in the ultimate sense, by 1844. The Millerites not only abandoned their earthly duties, they also jettisoned almost every other tenet of the faith as secondary. In the end they desired to be called "Adventists," which was the single thing that defined them. As the Second Coming becomes more of an obsession, it appears that those who do not believe the same way are somehow lacking spiritually. How could one ignore the arrival of the greatest event in history? Believers were no longer seen as Christians united under the cross, but as Millerites and non-Millerites divided only—but definitively—by their eschatology. The desire to separate from those who are less spiritual (and are even criticizing the very nature of the predictions that define the movement) becomes very appealing. Exclusivity leads to isolation, and once Christians are isolated from the fellowship of other believers, they have lost their connection to reality. To focus one's faith on one doctrine and to subordinate all others very easily leads to detrimental consequences.

Our hope is that we recognize that if all of this could happen to average, rational evangelicals like those attracted to Millerism 150 years ago, it could happen to us today. After beginning with such orthodox foundations, the Millerites lost their way, fixating on the Second Advent and becoming a cultlike, exclusive group. Many of them became disillusioned with the faith or adopted heretical views to avoid facing the unbearable reality that the beliefs they had put all their trust in were shown to be false.

5
Thy Kingdom Did Not Come
The Doomsday Mentality & Cognitive Dissonance

TIME ROLLS ON HIS RESISTLESS COURSE. WE ARE ONE MORE year down its rapid stream towards the ocean of eternity. We have passed what the world calls the last round of 1843; and already they begin to shout victory over us. Does your heart begin to quail? Are you ready to give up your blessed hope in the glorious appearing of Jesus Christ? or are you waiting for it, although it seems to us that it tarries? Let me say to you in the language of the blessed Book of God, "Although it tarry, wait for it; it will surely come, it will not tarry." Never has my faith been stronger than at this very moment.[1]

These words from a letter written by William Miller were published in late January 1844, less than two months before the deadline he had set for the Second Advent of Christ—March 21, 1844. With time running out, critics both secular and Christian increased their mocking of the movement. Notice the hope Miller wished to give his followers as he calls them to persevere in the midst of adversity. It would be tempting to turn and run. Miller declared, however, that his own faith had never been stronger. Ironically, his faith and the faith of most Millerites would grow even more sure once the March 21 date had come and passed without Christ's return. It seems unbelievable, but the greatest and quickest growth in the Millerite movement occurred *after* the prediction of Christ's return, on which the movement was based, failed. We will discuss why that happened in this chapter. As we shall see, though, the movement could not sustain the blow of a second failed prediction. The results were catastrophic for thousands of people who had put their trust in prognostications of Christ's return.

In the last chapter we saw how Millerism, which began as a parachurch, interdenominational, mainstream movement, whose leaders guarded against it becoming a sect, quickly began to break away from the evangelical community because of what was going on within, as well as outside, the movement. Millerites found new spiritual life in the movement while their home churches seemed to grow colder and to have little enthusiasm for the imminent Second Coming of Christ. Those outside the movement felt Millerites were rude in pushing their beliefs on others and were too extreme in elevating one doctrine above all of others. Some were concerned that Miller had actually set a date (or at least a time span) for Christ's return. Others said that his calculations were simplistic and that he approached the subject of eschatology in an unlearned fashion. The secular world, and perhaps some within the Christian community, thought Millerites were just a ridiculous bunch of fanatics who deserved the scorn they received. The Millerites felt ostracized amid the criticism; they had stepped outside normal societal and traditional religious standards. Perhaps to a greater degree, though, they believed they were the remnant that would hold fast to the truth and separate from the rest of civilization, which was now, in truly sectarian terms, viewed as Babylon, the realm of antichrist. With this separation came the severing of ties that bound Millerites to an accurate view of reality, leaving them vulnerable to the heretical behavior they were soon to display.

We believe the same bizarre phenomenon could reappear soon in our own day, given the parallel circumstances of the Millerites and those evangelicals today who believe that the beginning of the end of the world began in 1948 and that we are now living in the last generation. We discussed the possible implications of this belief in the last chapter. We would now like to discuss what might happen to Christians who take these views to their extremes. What ultimately happens to people who get caught up in millennial fever and separate themselves from the immoral and scoffing world around them as well as from their fellow believers? In the midst of this frenzy, what if these people start setting dates for the Second Coming and the Lord does not return? How will people react if the greatest event in human history does not occur when they think it will? We may find some answers by observing what happened to the Millerites a century ago and to other groups in our own time.

Reactions to Failed Prophecy

In the Millerites' experience, we find two key reactions that take place when millennial hopes are not fulfilled. The first and most obvious is that people become disillusioned with Christianity as a whole and, in some cases, question or actually abandon their spiritual convictions. They have put their trust in one primary doctrine, eschatology, with all others being subject to it. If they tie their beliefs to Christ returning by a particular date (or within a limited span of time) and that date passes without his appearing, their core faith, and not just their faith in the fulfillment of that event, may be questioned, if not abandoned. By the end of 1844 many Millerites were left in a world in which they were derided for their beliefs, cast off by everyone and everything that brought meaning to their lives and left at the edges of society with their faith shattered and with nothing left to hold onto. Some of the disillusioned were left without any spiritual moorings, while others joined alternative adventist groups, like the Shakers, in which they were warmly received and accepted.

The other, and more peculiar, reaction may have even more serious consequences than the first. It is in fact the polar opposite of the first.

Some millenarians, instead of becoming disillusioned and questioning their beliefs when the predicted date of Christ's return comes and passes, actually seem unaffected by the failed prediction and believe even more fervently that the prediction was somehow correct or will still be fulfilled. They psychologically relieve the stress caused by their disappointment by rationalizing away what actually happened. They are even prone to increase the proclamation of their beliefs and set a new date for Christ's return.[2] In hundreds of cases, Millerites followed and even exhibited fanatical behavior or adopted heretical doctrines in an effort to sustain their repression of what actually happened—Christ did not return when they believed he would. Failing to deal with this reality caused even more harm than facing the disillusionment and despair brought about by acknowledging the truth. Further, once this kind of rationalization is accepted, it becomes a permanent part of one's thinking.

We may again turn to the social sciences to shed light on why this phenomenon, known as cognitive dissonance, takes place. Leon Festinger is considered the leading expert and pioneer in applying cognitive dissonance to millenarian movements. In his *A Theory of Cognitive Dissonance,* Festinger explains that human beings usually strive for consistency (or consonance) in their beliefs (cognition). If one then acknowledges or does something that is inconsistent with his beliefs, he usually tries to rationalize the inconsistency (or dissonance) as being consistent with his beliefs instead of accepting the inconsistency at face value. If the rationalization process does not work and the inconsistency persists, one will feel uncomfortable. To alleviate this feeling, he will force himself to reduce the dissonance, attaining consonance, and avoid anything that would increase the dissonance.[3]

For example, members of a millenarian movement may set a date for the end of the world and the return of Christ. When the date passes and the prediction has not come true, they experience dissonance—the reality of things is inconsistent with their belief. They will also feel victimized by those who mock them for holding to such a seemingly odd belief. These circumstances will create great distress. They may accept that the prediction has failed and become greatly disillusioned. On the other hand, if they cannot accept the truth, they may attempt to relieve the uncomfortable feeling by rationalizing away the failure of the prediction: They may set a new date, explain why the first one was incorrect or claim that the prediction was fulfilled and provide an alternative interpretation to what happened. They will also tend to ignore or condemn anything that forces them to deal with the reality of the situation.

Further, Festinger claims that people who have made a commitment to a certain conviction, to the point of taking action that cannot be reversed, will, ironically, become even more convinced of the correctness of their conviction when presented with evidence that it is absolutely wrong.[4] He discusses five conditions under which this phenomenon occurs:

1. A belief must be held with deep conviction and it must have some relevance to action, that is, to what the believer does or how he behaves.

2. The person holding the belief must have committed himself to it; that is, for the sake of his belief, he must have taken some important action that is difficult to undo. In general, the more important such actions are, and the more difficult they are to undo, the greater is the individual's commitment to the belief.

3. The belief must be sufficiently specific and sufficiently concerned with the real world so that events may unequivocally refute the belief.

4. Such undeniable disconfirmatory evidence must occur and must be recognized by the individual holding the belief.[5]

Given these four conditions, we might expect that individuals would surrender their conviction. This will occur in many instances, but one further condition must be in place before people will hold onto a belief proved false.

5. The individual believer must have social support. . . . If . . . the believer is a member of a group of convinced persons who can support one another, we would expect the belief to be maintained and the believers to attempt to proselyte or to per-

suade nonmembers that the belief is correct.[6]

In the case of millenarian movements, the group must have set a date or a period of time within which Christ would return, giving details as to just what would take place. The commitment to the date must be held as important and is usually stated publicly. The commitment may also be cemented as a reaction to those outside the movement mocking such a decision.[7]

We do not have to stretch our imagination very far to see that this could happen today to those who believe we are definitely living in the last generation. Holding such a belief could lead to unorthodox behavior, including setting dates for Christ's return. When the date comes and passes, some who have become obsessed with a prediction of the Second Coming will find that their faith is crushed, and they will become disillusioned because they had a great deal of hope in that prediction. Others may find that their convictions are not easy to surrender. They will not be able to accept reality because to do so would devastate them. Those caught up in the doomsday mentality may not only rationalize away the failed prophecy and never come back to the truth (even when their false beliefs have been exposed), but they may also engage in even more heretical behavior to cover up what they cannot accept.

Instances of this have been noted throughout the history of the church, beginning in the second century with the Montanists. Several centuries later Anabaptist leader Melchior Hofmann predicted Christ would return and the world would end in 1533. His followers, known as the Melchiorites, renounced the world, paid off their debts, devoted themselves to spiritual contemplation and focused their attention on Strasbourg, the supposed New Jerusalem, in anticipation of the great event. When 1533 passed, the enthusiasm of the Melchiorites was not diminished but actually intensified. Hofmann disciple Jan Matthys renewed the mission of announcing Christ's return by sending out "apostles" in pairs from his stronghold in Amsterdam to proclaim that Enoch had come and the wicked would soon be judged. In a short time the zealous apostles baptized thousands of converts and won many in the cities of Holland.[8]

The Millerites

Perhaps the most fascinating demonstration of both responses to failed millennial hopes—disillusionment and the maintenance of a belief proved false—can be found in Millerism. The Millerite movement provides the best-documented case in history of the results of failed prophecy on mainstream, evangelical Christians.[9] Also, as stated before, the Millerites' profile and experiences so parallel those in our own day that we may look to them as perhaps the best historical example of what could happen to many evangelicals as the twenty-first century approaches.

It goes without saying that the tragic end of the Millerite movement was cast at its beginning when Miller calculated the Second Advent would take place "about the year 1843." Through 1842 he did not modify that open-ended prediction. On January 1, 1843, however, he published an outline of his teachings, concluding, "I am fully convinced that sometime between March 21st, 1843 and March 21st, 1844, . . . Christ will come, and bring all His saints with Him; and that then He will reward every man as his work shall be."[10] Miller claimed that he had never set a specific date for the Second Advent, yet he decided to set in motion a definitive time span in which he predicted it would take place. The seeds of disillusionment and cognitive dissonance had been planted.

As noted in the last chapter, Millerism's popularity increased exponentially throughout 1843. Large halls were rented in major metropolitan areas for weeks at a time, with the attendance at some meetings reaching into the thousands. Although its strength lay in the New England states, Millerism spread throughout the country, in established cities as well as frontier towns and villages. It was even capturing an international following; the movement was very strong in England, and there were confirmed reports that the message had reached such distant lands as Chile in South America. It seems unbelievable, but Miller called for the distribution of one million tracts by the end of 1843.[11]

As the self-imposed March 21, 1844, deadline neared, Miller seemed to doubt his prediction and rationalize its possible failure. He claimed that there could be a delay in Christ's coming for several reasons: the Lord might test the Millerites' faith; there might be errors in the chronology he used for the calculations; there were various ways of interpreting the Jewish calendar upon which the calculations were based.[12] Miller published statements that seemed to anticipate his prediction would not be fulfilled. The following broad and open-ended quote from one of Miller's editorials was published a month before the deadline, perhaps in an attempt to cover his tracks: "If we are mistaken in the time [referring to his March 21 prediction], we feel the fullest confidence that the event we have anticipated is the next great event in the world's history."[13] It seems from this that Miller was preparing his followers for a disappointment. After all, the "next great event in the world's history" could be months if not years away. Such ambiguities characterized other statements in the Millerite press; for example, "If Christ comes, as we expect, we will sing the song of victory soon; if not, we will watch, and pray, and preach until He comes, for soon our time, and all prophetic days, will have been filled."[14] That was published only two weeks before Christ's predicted return. Again, in how many ways could "soon" be interpreted?

The Millerites enthusiastically awaited the coming of March 21. One can imagine the excitement of being in the middle of a group of Christians who believed the Lord was coming back in only a matter of days. The Millerites were ready to be taken up. It would seem, then, that if the Lord did not return there would be a great sense of hopelessness among those who were waiting. Amazingly, in an overt display of cognitive dissonance, as March 21 came and passed, there was no sudden sense of disappointment among most Millerites. Only those who had a shallow commitment to the movement fell away— there was little disillusionment recorded among dedicated Millerites. The majority of them openly accepted their leader's rationale for the "delay" of the Lord's return.[15]

Ironically, once the Second Advent did not materialize, its nearness was felt more than ever. The First Disappointment created a new fervency and certainty where confusion would be expected. Millerite meetings were scheduled "Providence permitting" and "if time continue." Millerites only intensified their efforts by holding conferences and camp meetings, sending out itinerant speakers and distributing literature. Miller and Himes themselves set out west on speaking tours. The leaders hoped to maintain the ranks by pleading with Millerites not to give up their work, fearing a lack of commitment would produce a bad testimony before the scoffing world as well as a loss of influence in a movement that had attracted tens of thousands. On May 2, in a letter, Miller acknowledged his miscalculation, but in the same stroke tried to rally the troops: "I *confess my error,* and acknowledge *my disappointment;* yet I still believe that the day of the Lord is near, even at the door; and I exhort you, my brethren, to be watchful, and not let that day come upon you unawares."[16]

The excitement produced by the failed prediction was evident across the country. Himes commented during his tour, "I have never witnessed a stronger, more active faith. Indeed, the faith and confidence of the brethren in the prophetic word was never stronger. I find few, if any, who ever believed on Bible evidence, that are at all shaken in the faith; while others are embracing our views."[17] Himes reported that in Philadelphia a short crisis over the March 21 failure was past and the requests for Millerite lectures were greater than ever; in Cincinnati four thousand turned out on the first night of a lecture series there.[18] How does one explain this? How can people not only continue to hold to a belief that has been proved wrong but actually strengthen their efforts to spread this belief? It seems that it can only be understood in the context of cognitive dissonance. We will offer a full evaluation of this phenomenon below.

Millerites, renewed in their mission, thirsted for more specific details regarding Christ's return. Millerite speaker Samuel S. Snow provided them with what they wanted most—a new date for the Second Advent. Even before the March 21 deadline, Snow published his position that Miller's calculations were incorrect. Daniel's 2,300 prophetic days would not end until the autumn of 1844, he proclaimed. There was no explanation for this conclusion, and Miller and other leaders cautioned against setting another date, but the view became very popular given the heightened longing for

Christ's return prompted by Miller himself.[19]

In the summer of 1844 Snow preached extensively on his theory, and it was widely accepted on a grassroots level among Millerites. He even set a new date: October 22, 1844. Snow explained that his calculation reflected the manner in which the Karaite Jews rendered the Jewish year. October 22 would be the tenth day of the seventh month of the Jewish calendar, the Day of Atonement. Millerite leaders were still reluctant to accept Snow's rendering, desiring to ward off any new specific date setting, but there was so much popular support for it that they could not stop the surge. On October 6, even Miller himself, reluctant to ever set a specific date, accepted the October 22 calculation. Millerites went out from a camp meeting where Snow had spoken with a zeal that seemed to be unparalleled to that point. The new date was accepted enthusiastically by Millerites across the country.[20] As the editor of the *Advent Herald* put it, the leaders of the movement finally accepted Snow's view when they saw the fervency with which it was held by such large numbers—"to oppose it, or even to remain silent longer, seemed to us to be opposing the work of the Holy Spirit." The editor also observed, "At first the definite time was generally opposed; but there seemed to be an irresistible power attending its proclamation, which prostrated all before it. It swept over the land with the velocity of a tornado, and it reached hearts in different and distant places almost simultaneously, and in a manner which can be accounted for only on the supposition that God was [in] it."[21]

As the new deadline, October 22, drew near, Millerites felt ambivalent as to what to do with their few remaining days. If they went about their daily routines, they would be called hypocrites. If they left their normal lives and spent their remaining days proselytizing, they would be labeled fanatics. There seemed to be a movement among farmers in New England not to plow their fields or harvest their crops, as a sign of faith in the Lord's return. Some Millerites left their normal lives to prepare spiritually or to spend more time spreading the message. the *Midnight Cry* newspaper reported, "Many are leaving all, to go out and warn the brethren and the world. . . . [In New York City and Philadelphia] stores are being closed, and they preach in tones the world understands, though they may not heed it."[22] One shop owner in New York hung a sign in his window: "This shop is closed in honor of the King of kings, who will appear about the 20th of October. Get ready, friends, to crown Him Lord of all."[23] Millerites wanted to be fully prepared to stand before the heavenly throne. Several sold all their possessions to pay off their debts. Others confessed small as well as significant crimes they had been committed. Some Millerites were even rumored to be throwing away money. By most accounts, however, the majority of Millerites lived out their lives normally.[24]

As noted in the last chapter, the Millerites were savagely mocked in the secular press and criticized in the religious press. The heat intensified with the approach of October 22. Newspapers falsely reported that Millerites donned white "ascension robes" and climbed hills to be closer to Christ when he returned. In one of the nastiest broadsides, titled "Grand Ascension of the Miller Tabernacle: Miller in his Glory, Saints and Sinners in one great CONGLOMERATION," the Boston Millerite tabernacle is lifted off the ground, headed toward heaven, with Miller sitting on a millennial chart and Millerites, dressed in ascension robes, clinging to the tabernacle for dear life; those left behind reach up to go with them. Himes is held back by Satan, who is saying to him, "Joshua V., you must stay with me."[25]

The weekly *Advent Herald* announced in its October 16 issue that "we shall make no provision for issuing a paper for the week following."[26] On the day Christ was to return Millerites behaved in different ways. Most were in their homes, churches or meeting halls awaiting the Savior. Many meetings dispersed early and the Millerites went home quietly. The police ended the meetings early in New York City, however, because of threats from mobs. In Cincinnati a secular newspaper reporter was surprised not only at the number of Millerites assembled—about fifteen hundred—but also by the animated spirit they displayed in light of the coming of what he interpreted as a grave event. One cannot imagine the intense excitement that must have coursed through the Millerites' veins. Many had been waiting for years; their faith had been tested in March and they had been proven trustworthy. Their long journey was over; their diligent work complete. Now the Lord would return; they would meet him face to face.[27] The great day became known as the Great Disappointment. As they awoke on October 23, most Millerites lapsed into despair as they found that the Lord had not returned; the glorious expectation was once again not fulfilled. Because the fervency generated after the first failure had run so high, the depths of despondency after the second could not be measured. The pathos one feels in their testimonies is considerable. Luther Boutelle, a Millerite lecturer who later became a leader of the Advent Christian Church, wrote:

But the 22nd of October passed, making unspeakably sad the faithful and longing ones; but causing the unbelieving and wicked to rejoice. All was still. No *Advent Herald;* no meetings as formerly. Everyone felt lonely, with hardly a desire to speak to anyone. Still in the cold world! No deliverance—the Lord not come! No words can express the feelings of disappointment of a true Adventist then. Those only who experienced it can enter into the subject as it was. It was a humiliating thing, and we all felt it alike. All were silent, save to inquire, "Where are we?" and "What next?" All were housed and searching their Bibles to learn what to do. In some few places they soon began to come together to watch for some development of light, relative to our disappointment.[28]

These sentiments are echoed by Hiram Edson, a farmer, who joined a group that formed after the Great Disappointment which later became known as the Seventh-day Adventists:

Our fondest hopes and expectations were blasted, and such a spirit of weeping came over us as I never experienced before. It seemed that the loss of all earthly friends could have been no comparison. We wept, and wept, till the day dawn.

I mused in my own heart, saying, My advent experience has been the richest and brightest of all my christian experience. If this had proved a failure, what was the rest of my christian experience worth? Has the Bible proved a failure? Is there no God—no heaven—no golden home city—no paradise? Is all this but a cunningly devised fable? Is there no reality to our fondest hopes and expectation of these things? And thus we had something to grieve and weep over, if all our fond hopes were lost. And as I said, we wept till the day dawn.[29]

In the midst of the emotional turmoil caused by the Great Disappointment, Millerites also faced physical persecution. Mobs not only taunted them but also broke into Millerite gatherings and assaulted those assembled. Millerite meeting places were vandalized and two New York tabernacles, in Ithaca and Danville, were actually destroyed.[30]

A pall of disillusionment covered everyone in the movement. Despite Himes's undaunted efforts to keep Millerism going (he had the Millerite newspapers publishing again within weeks), the movement collapsed under the weight of the unfulfilled advent and the public's relentless scoffing and derision. Millerite congregations quickly fell to a small fraction of their peak numbers; for example, in Oswego, New York, out of a hundred members a mere fifteen remained. There were no new members and no new converts. But the Millerites faced an even greater problem: Many had sold everything to prepare for the Second Advent and had no earthly possessions left. This was such a widespread problem that Himes called for a major drive to assist these destitute members and pleaded with those who had already started talking about setting another date to desist.[31]

Barkun notes that most Millerites reacted in one of three ways to the Great Disappointment. There were those who were so disillusioned they left the movement completely and attempted to return to their denominational churches. Others wanted nothing to do with traditional, Millerite adventism, but desired to be among people who shared deep millennial convictions expressed in unconventional (and usually unorthodox) ways. These Millerites joined one of several utopian communities. Those going in a third direction attempted to rationalize away the Great Disappointment and continue on the Millerite path.[32] We wish to discuss these three groups in more detail.

The majority of Millerites quickly left the movement and suffered substantially from their disenchantment. Some even became embittered and turned against the movement. Miller wrote to a friend in

December, "The same ones and many more who were crying for mercy two days before were now mixed with the rabble and mocking, scoffing, and threatening in the most blasphemous manner."[33] Most returned to their churches, but a significant portion were not welcomed back, falling under the discipline of their denominations. Methodists and Baptists even made Millerism the scapegoat of their quickly declining membership figures in the mid-1840s. In fact, scholars have noted that the cause of the declining numbers may be found more in hotly debated social issues like slavery and the fact that the churches were losing members because the denominations themselves were expelling Millerites.[34] Ernest R. Sandeen offers these words in summarizing his discussion of the movement: "The failure of his [Miller's] predictions disillusioned most of his followers and marked the whole millenarian cause, rightly or wrongly, with the stigma of fanaticism and quackery."[35]

For certain Millerites the effects of the Great Disappointment were devastating. The secular press reported that some of them had committed suicide or murder or had gone insane over the Great Disappointment. Nichol has done a convincing job of showing that the murder and suicide stories were totally exaggerated and has systematically dismissed the idea that Millerism caused madness.[36] But one thorough study of the psychological effects of Millerism found that an astonishing 170 patients were admitted to American asylums for causes "related to Millerism." It should be noted that these patients were diagnosed according to their behavioral symptoms, not their religious convictions, so the causes of their symptoms were not automatically attributed to Millerism. Further, during the 1840s, discussion of Millerism and its relation to mental illness began appearing regularly in psychological journals. Amariah Brigham, one of the leading nineteenth-century authorities on insanity, went so far as to state that the public's health was threatened more by Millerism than by either yellow fever or cholera.[37]

Other Millerites found it impossible to return to the traditional denominations. They wished to be defined primarily by the adventist convictions they had embraced in Millerism, but they were either not welcome in their home churches or they felt returning to them would be a step back. They sought to express their faith in a small community of like-minded people, so they joined sympathetic sects, such as the Shakers, which focused their teachings on the Second Advent. Millerites also found the emphasis on personal and communal piety a welcome relief from the infighting that had come to characterize Millerism. It should be noted, however, that the Shakers, the Oneida Community and several of the other utopian sects were heretical in many of their beliefs. For instance, the Shakers claimed that their leader, Ann Lee, was divinely inspired just as Jesus had been divinely inspired on earth; therefore, she was "Christ's Second Appearing." This and other unbiblical beliefs did not bother some Millerites because the communities were successful and harmonious, unlike Millerism, which had been decimated and discredited. The appeal of these communities must have been substantial; for example, in 1845, more than half of the 144 members of the Shaker community in Whitewater, Ohio, were former Millerites.[38]

These responses are certainly worth exploring, but we feel the third group is the most interesting. One may account for disillusionment and bitterness. Joining a group with questionable beliefs may even be plausible for those who wished to remain adventists while distancing themselves from Millerism. How does one explain, though, the actions of those who choose to try to sustain a movement whose central tenet has twice been proven false? A significant portion of the Millerites did just that by rationalizing what had happened—or didn't happen—on March 21 and October 22. Chief among the true believers was Miller himself, who wrote, "Although I have been twice disappointed, I am not yet cast down or discouraged. . . . I have now much more evidence that I do believe in God's Word; and although surrounded with enemies and scoffers, yet my mind is perfectly calm, and my hope in the coming of Christ is as strong as ever."[39] One is astounded by the extent to which Miller refuses to accept reality. How could he cling to his theories after his own prediction and another he endorsed had been proven wrong? Again, the best explanation is found in the theory of cognitive dissonance: Not only will people rationalize away something that runs contrary to their cherished beliefs, but they will also intensify their efforts to proselytize for their cause. How else can one account for the fact that by one estimate there were still as many as fifty thousand people who claimed to be Millerites in 1849, five years after the Great Disappointment?[40]

Similar to the reaction that followed the First Disappointment, several theories began to emerge among the remnant of Millerites who rationalized the Great Disappointment, most of which are demonstrations of the extent to which the doomsday mentality dominates those who fall prey to it. Some people went to great lengths to avoid the truth so that they could hold onto their false beliefs. Millerite leader George Storrs claimed that some strange force he called "mesmerism" adversely affected the thinking of Millerites. Storrs failed to elaborate on the actual nature of that force. Another said the delay of the Second Advent was indeed of God; it was his method of separating true from false believers. Elon Galusha held that the Great Disappointment was due to human error; the calculation was simply wrong. Amazingly, some Millerites, including Miller's son, George, insisted that God would only bless them if they set a new date for the Second Advent. A plethora of predictions followed: November 10, 1844; March 1845; April 8-24, 1845; autumn 1846. Some set several new dates as each prediction failed.[41]

An entirely different school of thought emerged alongside the ones already mentioned. Certain Millerites believed something actually did take place on October 22, 1844, but that it happened in the spiritual, not the physical, realm. Some believed Christ came to earth spiritually to judge who was righteous and who was not. This concept caught on quickly and found many followers. One theory stated that Christ cleansed the heavenly temple, referred to in Daniel 8:14, paving the way for the Second Advent. Other spiritualizers, who came to be known as the "shut door adventists," took a much tougher stand. They proposed that on October 22, Christ judged all of humankind in heaven, separating the saved and unsaved, and shut the door of redemption on the latter. The final judgment of the righteous and damned had been completed. Many spiritualizers believed all true

Christians had been sanctified; unfortunately, this state of perfection led in some cases to licentious and cultlike behavior, including illicit sexual practices and bizarre forms of brainwashing. Ironically, it was these rather radical spiritualizers who were the most effective in winning over those Millerites who remained faithful. Other aberrant doctrines began to find an audience among the Millerites desperately looking for an answer to pacify the dissonance they were experiencing. Many found themselves adopting beliefs in such things as soul sleep, annihilation of the lost and the seventh-day Sabbath.[42]

In April 1845 Miller and the other more moderate leaders held a conference in Albany, New York, to solidify the fragmented movement and work out a strategy for keeping the radical spiritualizers and their bizarre beliefs in check. The conference unified the moderates but only further alienated the extremists, leaving Millerism splintered into innumerable sects. It was obvious at the conference that Miller had lost prominence as a leader, being held responsible for both of the failed predictions as well as being criticized for adopting and then renouncing the shut door view. Miller was constantly ill and depressed, the stress and guilt produced by the failure of the movement that bore his name having taken its toll. With Himes by his side, Miller died on December 30, 1849, at the age of 68.[43]

Millerism did not die with its founder, but it had shattered into several pieces. Those splinter groups that remained found the basis of their existence in attempts to rationalize the Great Disappointment. Perhaps the most successful of these groups is now known as the Seventh-day Adventists and today boasts more than 3.5 million members worldwide.[44] Just two months after the Great Disappointment, a seventeen-year-old Millerite from Maine, Ellen Gould Harmon, had an apocalyptic vision in which faithful adventists were ascending to heaven to meet Christ. Certain adventists interpreted this as a charge from God to remain faithful in watching for his Son's imminent return. Harmon soon acquired popularity as a prophetess as more visions followed. In 1846 she married James White, a former school teacher and Millerite preacher. James and Ellen G. White, along with Millerite leader Joseph Bates (who accepted the necessity of Sabbath worship on Saturday soon after the Great Disappointment and convinced the Whites to do so too), became the driving force behind the group known as the Sabbatarian Adventists.[45]

In rationalizing the Great Disappointment, the Sabbatarian Adventists accepted the spiritualized explanation of Millerite Hiram Edson, which he formulated the day after the Great Disappointment. According to Edson, the "cleansing of the sanctuary" referred to in Daniel 8:14, the focus of Miller's calculations, actually did take place on October 22, 1844, in heaven. Christ entering the heavenly sanctuary symbolized how he was "blotting out" sins, not just forgiving them. With this last task accomplished in heaven, the stage was set for Christ's return to earth.[46] Ellen G. White added another dimension to rationalizing the delay of Christ's return. In one of her visions, the warning of the third angel in Revelation 14:9-11 against worshiping the beast was related directly to Sabbath worship. That is, White maintained that Christ's return had been delayed because Christians were not keeping the Ten Commandments, particularly the fourth.[47]

Under the charismatic leadership of Ellen G. White, the new movement attracted followers quickly, many of whom were former Millerites. In the *Adventist Review and Herald,* James White documented his wife's spiritual experiences and continued the adventist emphasis on Christ's imminent return. By 1850, the beliefs of the group became solidified. The Sabbatarian Adventists

> accepted the Bible—and the Bible only—as their rule of faith and duty; the law of God as immutable (including the binding obligation to observe the seventh-day Sabbath); the imminent personal Advent of Christ; the conditional immortality of the soul; and the ministry of Christ in the heavenly sanctuary after 1844 in the blotting out of sins.[48]

The Sabbatarian Adventists took on a new name, the Seventh-day Adventists (SDAs), and focused their efforts in a new direction. In trying to cure her bad health, Ellen G. White began regulating her diet. Nutrition quickly became a spiritual matter. White joined forces in Battle Creek, Michigan, with Dr. John Harvey Kellogg, who became famous for his cereals. The SDAs are still known for their work in nutrition, health care and mental health, and they have for the most part become part of mainstream American culture. Yet they still hold on to many of their original doctrines adopted in the days following the Great Disappointment, some of which have caused critics to declare they are not orthodox in their beliefs. For instance, the doctrinal statement they adopted in 1980 still espouses soul sleep, the 1844 cleansing of the heavenly sanctuary and the necessity of Saturday Sabbath worship.[49]

We have seen how the Millerites separated from their fellow believers and society as a whole as the effects of the doomsday mentality overwhelmed them. We have also seen that this phenomenon led formerly strong evangelicals to leave the faith completely, join unorthodox utopian groups and adopt heretical beliefs to avoid the pain caused by their unfulfilled prophecies. We want now to analyze the movement, utilizing the theory of cognitive dissonance to help us understand what happened to them.

1. The Millerites' adventist tenets were held with deep conviction and directly affected their daily lives. What could be more important to an evangelical than knowing that Christ was returning within a matter of months or even weeks? Eschatology became the doctrine around which all others revolved.

2. The Millerites not only held to the teachings of their leader with great assurance, they also made a commitment to the movement in such a way that it could not be undone without great embarrassment. To back away from identifying with such a bold prediction would be very difficult to do. Their devotion became quite exclusive: Millerites eventually felt a need to leave their churches and fellowship only with those in the movement. On the one hand, they were ostracized by fellow evangelicals for their belligerent and dogmatic manner; on the other, the Millerites ultimately identified those with whom they had previously worshiped as enemies of Christ, destined for judgment. Their commitment was further solidified by defying those who mocked the movement. Their devotion increased in proportion to the movement's taking on the characteristics of a sect.

3. Miller's prediction was kept ambiguous through 1842. Until that

time he said the Second Advent would occur "about" 1843. At the beginning of that year he clarified his findings and proclaimed the event would take place between March 21, 1843, and March 21, 1844. It is odd to think that Miller disliked those who set dates for the last days and said he refused to do so himself, yet with his prediction he made it quite clear that Christ had to return by March 21, 1844. Samuel Snow held no such pretensions in making the October 22, 1844, prediction, and he convinced the Millerites that the Second Advent would occur on that date.

4. It is also clear that the predictions proved false: Christ did not return by March 21, 1844, or on October 22, 1844.

5. There was more than adequate support for Millerites from fellow members. Even in the despair of the Great Disappointment, many held fast to their convictions, meeting together for prayer and comfort. They formed elaborate and often outrageous theories as to what had happened and mapped out strategies for what to do next.

The essential characteristics of the phenomenon are apparent. We then must ask why cognitive dissonance occurs. As discussed previously, people try to maintain consistency, or consonance, in their belief systems, or cognition. The Millerites certainly felt they were consistent in their beliefs. They were indeed orthodox evangelicals in most respects, with the obvious exception of their eschatological views. They felt their convictions were based on Scripture and went to great lengths to prove so.

When something is introduced into the belief system that does not fit, however, dissonance occurs, which causes discomfort.[50] Pressure builds to reduce the dissonance and thus relieve the discomfort. One may try to change part of the dissonance, acquire more knowledge that supports the consonance and thus lessens the effects of the dissonance, or ignore or overlook the significance of the dissonance. For any of these options to work, there must be support from like-minded people to confirm the commitment to the belief. The Millerites were exposed to extreme dissonance as the Second Coming of Christ failed to occur two separate times when they believed it would. One can imagine the pain they must have felt as the focus of all their work and dedication was crushed. Anyone would immediately attempt to reduce such pain, perhaps by rejecting the belief that had been proven false. Some Millerites did exactly that—they left the movement quickly.

For so many, however, the commitment to the cause had been so strong that any other solution would be more desirable than admitting the predictions had been wrong. It would be in fact less painful to withstand the dissonance than jettison the belief. At this point, it is impossible for the dissonance to be reduced by forfeiting the conviction. Because of the nature of the movement, committed Millerites found it impossible to abandon its core tenet. Alternatives needed to be found. After March 21, 1844, Miller apologized for being wrong in his exact calculation but sought to reduce the dissonance he experienced by proclaiming the Second Coming was closer than ever and would occur at any moment. After October 22, 1844, the rationalizations became more grand and bizarre because the dissonance that came with a second disappointment was overwhelming. So, one finds an abundance of far-fetched scenarios: Some strange "mesmerism" affected Millerite thinking; God was really testing their faith; the calculation was wrong, the next one would certainly be right; something did happen on October 22, only it happened in heaven; God had shut the final door on everyone who was not in the Millerite camp.

Rationalization, however, is not enough for those believers who are most committed and thus have the most to lose from their cherished belief being proven false. For them it is still too painful to face the truth that they were wrong, that they had put their hope in a false prophecy and that their work was in vain. Yet, they may still decrease the dissonance in one significant way: If they can somehow persuade other people that their beliefs are correct, then perhaps they are indeed correct. The greater the number of people that are persuaded, the more likely it is that there is something right about the belief system. They would be vindicated. Who would, in fact, commit themselves to something that is false? New converts weaken the power and the pain of dissonance.

If this is true, we may then understand why Millerites increased their efforts at proselytizing and promoting their doctrines after the March 21 and October 22 predictions did not come true. If they were able to persuade people that they were still right, the effects of the dissonance they felt would be diminished. This possibly explains why the proselytizing after the Great Disappointment was most successful in unorthodox and heretical sects. If people could still be attracted to a group that required unusually high levels of exclusive commitment and faithfully held to strange doctrines, would it not be obvious that that group's convictions were right?

We fear the same type of thinking could affect those evangelicals today who seem obsessed with the Second Coming and believe we must be living in the last generation. Separating from fellow believers leaves one vulnerable to taking on heretical doctrines, including setting dates for the Lord's return. What will happen to these people when their prophecies are unfulfilled? Some will become disillusioned, but others will maintain their false beliefs because facing them is too agonizing. We fear evangelicals may become vulnerable to unbiblical beliefs and practices which would be very difficult to surrender.

Evangelicals might claim that what happened to the Millerites could never happen today to their fellow believers. They would find it hard to believe that modern-day evangelicals would set dates for the Second Coming. It seems even more unlikely to them that evangelicals would deny that any such predictions were wrong, once they did not come to pass. We will see, however, that there are parallels between the Millerites and several contemporary phenomena. When faced with the fact that their predictions have been proven erroneous, some people rationalize away the truth, refusing to deal with reality, and cling to their false prophecies. We find once again in the theory of cognitive dissonance the best rationale for explaining the thinking and behavior that emerge in the following present-day examples.

Recalculating the Last Generation

As we have discussed previously, certain evangelicals believe that the end of the world commenced in 1948 when Israel once again became a nation; that is, they believe that since that time we have been living in the last generation before the Second Coming. Just as Miller believed he was not setting dates because he predicted Christ's return within a time span, not on a specific date, modern-day prognosticators think they are not setting dates. Yet, they declare the end will come one generation after 1948. They then offer various calculations for the length of a generation: thirty, forty or one hundred years. They are clearly saying that Christ must return by 1978, 1988 or 2048, even though they claim they do not set dates. This certainly seems to be date setting, but they do not believe it is.

One such example of this thinking is found in Edgar C. Whisenant's bestselling booklet, *88 Reasons Why the Rapture Will Be in 1988*.[51] When 1988 passed without Christ's return, how did Whisenant handle his false prediction? One might think that he would admit his error and desist from making more predictions. Instead, he published a sequel, *The Final Shout: Rapture Report 1989, 1990, 1991, 1992, 1993* . . . (Note how the author allows, even in the title of his book, for the possibility that he will be wrong again.) In the sequel Whisenant states the following about his 1988 prediction: "I was mistaken! I now believe that Rosh-Hashanah, 1988 was the shout, 'the Bridegroom cometh,' as spoken of in Mat. 25:1-13. This shout gave God's people a one-year awakening, or preparation period, so they would be ready as was the wise bride who had prepared her light to meet her groom (Jesus)."[52] One is astounded by the way in which the author seems to refuse to accept the facts of the situation—his prediction was simply wrong. He rationalizes his error by offering a rather preposterous explanation for why Christ did not return by the end of 1988. It is even more astounding that the publisher of *88 Reasons* states in a letter that opens the book, "We pray that as a servant of our Lord, Jesus Christ, you will want to alert to others [sic] as we have alerted you. No harm can come from sounding the alarm. . . . We have seen many souls brought to Jesus after reading this book."[53] It seems that the publisher is saying that the book, even if its predictions are plainly false, is legitimized and justified because it can be used as an evangelistic tool. After examining what happened to the Millerites and others like them, we see that there may be a great deal of harm that can come from false prophecies.

Other prognosticators who predicted the Lord's return in 1988 simply shifted the beginning of the last generation from 1948 to 1967. Their rationale is as follows: Jesus promised that the generation that witnessed the restoration of the Jewish people to their homeland would not pass away until "all these things" (the signs of the times), including his return, took place. Although Israel became a nation again in 1948, it was not until the Six Day War in 1967 that they reclaimed their holy city, Jerusalem. Oropeza finds that prognosticators allow for certain flexibility in their predictions in case they fail and also to fend off criticism that they are setting dates. So, the last generation may be calculated as thirty, forty or one hundred years and may begin in 1948, 1967, 1994 (the signing of the peace accords between Israel and the Palestinian Liberation Organization) or maybe even 1917 (the Balfour Declaration, in which the British government promised the Jews a homeland in Palestine). Future events in the Middle East will probably prompt even more recalculations.[54]

It is the doomsday mentality that allows one to accept this kind of thinking. We saw this in the Millerites, many of whom reset the date for Christ's coming many times after the Great Disappointment. They were simply unable to accept the reality that they had committed themselves to a movement whose core tenet was untrue. If one accepts that we are, without question, living in the last generation, it would be difficult to resist setting a date for the Second Coming. Once those predictions are made and they are proved false, one is put in a precarious spot. Since the prediction of Christ's return and the actual event have been joined in one's thinking, how does one renounce one without renouncing the other? It is less stressful to deny that the prediction was wrong—one simply recalculates to ease the pain. Rationalizing a false belief is easier than accepting that it was wrong.

Redefining the Soviet Union

For years doomsday prognosticators have claimed that the Soviet Union was the enemy from the North referred to in Ezekiel 38—39 that will swoop down to attack Israel in the last days.[55] This may have made sense when the Soviet Union was a major superpower, but how can this be the case now that the once-mighty empire has collapsed? Hal Lindsey, an author who has written a great deal on the subject, has changed his last days scenario in light of the Soviet Union's fall. It should be noted that Lindsey is certainly not alone in changing his analysis of the Soviet Union's role in biblical prophecy. Boyer states that many prognosticators amend their interpretations as political circumstances change and as their predictions are proven untrue or highly unlikely to be fulfilled. He portrays the popular prophecy writers as rather syncretistic in that they include new global events within their prophetic schemes, oftentimes ignoring the fact that the new developments contradict their former interpretations. Boyer finds a clear demonstration of this in shifting views on the role of the former Soviet Union and the world of Islam in popular prophetic literature.[56]

Lindsey states in his recent book *Planet Earth—2000 A.D.* that although the ailing Russia may no longer be a superpower, it will become a dominant force in world affairs because of its nuclear arsenal and will form an alliance with Iran, the leader of the newest major threat to Israel—Islam. This union will be made for two primary reasons: (1) because Russia needs money to survive and revive its empire, it will sell nuclear arms to Iran; and (2) the strong Islamic presence in the former Soviet republics will force Moscow to enter into a peace pact with Tehran. Together, at Iran's insistence, these two nations will attack Israel, thus fulfilling Ezekiel 38:2-6. In fact, Persia (Iran) will be the "hook in the jaw of Magog" that will draw Magog (Russia) into the ultimate war with Israel, Armageddon (Ezek 38:4). The theory is that because of the alliance, Iran, the dominant partner, will force Russia to join in an attack on Israel.[57]

Twenty-five years ago, Lindsey published *The Late Great Planet Earth,* which has sold millions of copies. In that book he describes in detail the two-flank assault the mighty Soviet forces will make on Israel—a land invasion from the north and an amphibious assault from the Mediterranean Sea. (He saw the buildup of Russian ships in the Mediterranean as a possible sign of the imminence of Armageddon.)

The Russians will double-cross their allies in the Islamic Arab confederacy, Lindsey theorized, but the Red Army will be destroyed by nuclear weapons deployed by the antichrist, who will lead the revived Roman Empire. This was all well and good for 1970, when the book was published, but drastic changes on the global political scene have forced Lindsey and others to change their interpretations that they had so much confidence in years ago.

So, how does Lindsey deal with the collapse of a major player in his predictions regarding the last days? He simply changes the story and the roles of the players. For instance, in 1970 Lindsey portrayed Iran as the pawn of the powerful Soviets, who force the "Persians" to ally with them to gain easy military access to the Middle East. In Lindsey's latest interpretation, however, the roles are reversed. Here the Russians crawl to Iran to make an alliance in search of financial help and fearing the Islamic presence in Russia. It is then the Russians who are dragged into a war with Israel because of Iran's power. Further, since the great Cold War Soviet Empire has fallen, it now seems ridiculous to think that Russia could pull off such things as mounting an invasion on the Middle East, much less one on two fronts.[58]

Lindsey anticipates reader confusion regarding such seemingly contradictory predictions: "But, Hal, you might ask, weren't you surprised by the crumbling of the Soviet Union? Isn't that an event that runs counter to biblical prophecy? Hasn't the Soviet Union's power been somewhat diminished?"[59] Lindsey explains that the Soviet Union, the supposed great bear to the north that would attempt to devour Israel, had to collapse in order to fulfill Scripture. This may seem like an obvious contradiction to the position Lindsey held previously, but to him it apparently is not. He states that under Mikhail Gorbachev the Soviet Union was about to take over all of Europe. (One might wonder how an empire that was about to fall and unable to control even its own satellite nations could take over Europe, but that is not explained.) Lindsey writes, "The collapse of the Soviet state was absolutely necessary to the fulfillment of biblical prophecy. The old Soviet Union was on a collision course with world domination.

Only the unforseen [sic] internal breakup of the Soviet Union could have prevented that eventuality. But world domination—as Ezekiel makes clear—*was never in the script for Russia!*"[60]

We do not deny that Russia and Iran could enter into an alliance with each other. After all, Russia has tried to sell nuclear weapons to Iran. It needs to be noted, however, that an alliance could be formed—and broken—between any number of nations in these turbulent and unpredictable times. The point we wish to make is that it seems difficult for those who predicted the Soviet Union would be the great enemy to the north that would swarm over Israel to acknowledge the fact that the empire is no more. Instead, they amend their interpretations to fit the current scene. Lindsey offers a concluding remark: "Yes, the Evil Empire may be gone, but Russia's role in the endtimes scenario remains the same. The mainstream media may not be tracking developments in Russia with much scrutiny and depth or giving them the attention they deserve, but, behind the scenes, there are momentous and profound events taking place in Moscow. The great bear may not look as dangerous as it once did, but looks can be deceiving."[61] Clearly Lindsey is rationalizing the error of predicting that a great Soviet military machine would invade Israel on two fronts and then be powerful enough to break its alliance with an Arab confederacy. He avoids dealing with the reality of the false prediction by saying now that the Soviet collapse was inevitable. We wonder how future events will once again change the theories of prognosticators.

David Koresh and the Branch Davidians

Although David Koresh was not an evangelical, the Branch Davidians are an offshoot of the Seventh-day Adventists. Koresh was, then, a spiritual descendant of William Miller. Unfortunately, the consequences of the Millerite false prophecies reached far beyond what anyone could have imagined. Miller never dreamed that one of his heirs would start a cult, engage in clearly abusive and perverted practices, claim to be Jesus Christ himself and take the lives of his followers and himself in an apocalyptic inferno. It is also interesting to see in the Branch Davidians clear demonstrations of people ignoring reality when certain prophecies are proved false. On April 19, 1993, the world watched in horror as the compound of the Branch Davidian cult was engulfed in flames. The Waco conflagration claimed the lives of Koresh and seventy-five to eighty-five of his followers, including some twenty-five children. Perhaps it appeared to the Branch Davidians that Koresh's prophecy had come true: As the Lamb would open the sixth judgment seal of Revelation 6:12, 17, his death was calculated to invoke the wrath of God on the world.[62] In reality, however, the death of Koresh and his disciples will be remembered not as a catalyst for the apocalypse but as the tragic end that often results when a group of people fail to think for themselves and follow instead the dictates of a delusional charismatic leader.

But why did Koresh's disciples follow him to their deaths? It seems that at least two key moments in the experience of the commune give us some insight. First, from 1988 on, Vernon Howell (Koresh's name before he had it legally changed in 1990) taught that he was "the Lamb" mentioned in the book of Revelation. He held this belief with deep conviction, perhaps because with it he could claim authority over the members of his cult and, particularly, command sexual power over its women.[63] Howell was apparently unaware, however, that the term he applied to himself, "the Lamb," is actually a reference to Jesus Christ. Revelation 4, 5, 19 and 20 make that clear. Marc Breault, a one-time follower of Koresh, pointed out the blatant contradiction to Koresh in a teaching session. When the issue was exposed, Koresh realized that his authority was summarily being refuted by the biblical evidence, that is, that the Lamb is Christ. He had to make a quick decision, and so he proclaimed that since he was the Lamb of Revelation, he must be Jesus Christ. David Bunds, who escaped from the compound, writes of this incident:

> Vernon was pressured, forced to make a decision. He either had to deny he was the Lamb or say he was Jesus. See, he couldn't stay where he was. But what he did was he said he was Jesus. . . . He wasn't gonna deny it . . . that means he wouldn't have been able to have the wives. The entire justification for him taking the women

was that he was the Lamb. . . . If he wasn't the Lamb, then that whole thing fell apart.[64]

Howell legally changed his name two years after this incident, taking on monikers of two of the greatest kings in the Old Testament, David and Koresh (which is Hebrew for Cyrus, that is, Cyrus the Great, the Medo-Persian king who freed the Jews from the Babylonian captivity and allowed them to return to Jerusalem). Koresh believed he was greater than both David and Cyrus. In a letter to Seventh-day Adventists, Koresh wrote, "I am the Son of God . . . the Immanuel. . . . My Name is the Word of God. . . . I Am all the prophets: all of them. . . . I have come in a way contrary to your preconceived ideas. . . . I Am the Word and you do not know Me."[65] Unfortunately, Koresh's followers supported his position despite their better judgment.

A second decisive moment in which the Branch Davidians at Waco refused to face the truth is found in their fiery demise. Though debate has raged both in and out of court over the origin of the blaze that destroyed the compound and killed its members, there is now compelling evidence that Koresh himself started the fire that turned the Branch Davidian compound into a funeral pyre. The data have been acquired from survivors of the fire, loyal followers of Koresh who still believe he was right, and from handwritten notes by Koresh and some of his disciples. One may conclude that Koresh believed that he was destined to fulfill a number of biblical apocalyptic texts, including Isaiah 4:4-5; Jeremiah 50:24, 32; Joel 2:1-5; Amos 8:9; Nahum 2:3-5 and Revelation 6:12, 17. Koresh taught that he was the Lamb of Revelation and that his death would be a catalyst for the unleashing of the divine judgment of the sixth seal of Revelation 6:12, 17, which will fall upon unbelievers. Using passages like Jeremiah 50:24, 32 and Joel 2:1-5, which speak of God sending fire upon the faithful believers' enemies, Koresh believed and taught that God's method of judging the enemies of the Branch Davidians would be by fire.[66]

Koresh went one step further, however, by applying Isaiah 4:4-5 to his followers as well. That text states, "The Lord will wash away the filth of the women of Zion; . . . by a spirit of judgment and a spirit of fire. Then the LORD will create over all of Mount Zion and over those who assemble there a cloud of smoke by day and a glow of flaming fire by night; over all the glory will be a canopy." We now know that Koresh interpreted this passage to mean that the fire God sent against the enemies of the Branch Davidians would also engulf them, except that the effect for them would be that it would kill off their old nature ("the Lord will wash away the filth of the women of Zion . . . by a spirit of fire") and transform them into flaming, glorified individuals ("a glow of flaming fire . . . over all the glory will be a canopy"). In other words, the fire would purify and glorify Koresh and his followers while destroying their enemies.[67]

We now know that when the tanks attacked the compound on April 19, 1993, Koresh interpreted that to be the fulfillment of Nahum 2:3-5, which speaks of the "chariots" of Israel's enemies raging in the streets, seeming to be like torches. In fact, a member of the Koresh cult, Robyn Bunds, had written the word "tanks" over the word "chariots" in Nahum 2:3-4 in her Bible. Koresh undoubtedly believed that, at the moment of an attack, God would destroy the tanks by fire. In fact, Nahum 2:13 reads, " 'I am against you,' declares the LORD Almighty, 'I will burn up your chariots in smoke.' "[68]

Finally, although the government's tanks attacked the Davidian compound at 6 a.m. on April 19, 1993, the fires did not break out until sometime between seven minutes before and five minutes after noon. The reason for this is to be found in Amos 8:9, " 'In that day,' declares the Sovereign LORD, 'I will make the sun go down at noon and darken the earth in broad daylight.' " Robyn Bunds's own notes in her Bible next to this passage, "DEATH OF CYRUS," that is, David Koresh, illuminate this text. It seems clear that Koresh planned the end to come at noon because he believed that the heavenly transformation of himself and his followers—and the judgment of his enemies—by fire at that precise time would be the fulfillment of Amos 8:9. The explosion that preceded an enormous fireball jolted the compound, perhaps also in fulfillment of Koresh's prediction that an earthquake would come as the end approached.[69]

We can clearly see that in both of these instances, Koresh and his followers ignored the truth in order to maintain a false belief. Koresh certainly did not want to deny that he was the Lamb in Revelation: His authority over the group would have been questioned and he may have had to give up his perverted sexual practices. His followers did not want to surrender this belief either, perhaps because they did not want to look like fools for having followed such a liar or perhaps because they simply believed that Koresh would never betray them in such a fashion. What was the result of this irrational choice? Koresh proclaimed himself to be Jesus Christ and his followers believed him.[70]

The same dynamics were at work on the day the compound was destroyed. Koresh told his people the fire that was to come would devour their enemies but purify them. It is hard to accept that anyone would believe such a thing, but, again, if people are convinced that their leader is Jesus Christ himself, they will find it hard to argue with anything he says. Koresh very easily read present circumstances back into the biblical text because his followers allowed him to. Even more astounding than all of this is the fact that a handful of Davidians in Waco, some of whom survived the inferno, still remain faithful to Koresh. It is said of these people that they continue to look forward to the day when their messiah—David Koresh—and his slain disciples will return in glory. Only then, they believe, will justice finally be served on those who opposed God and his followers. How can people who have so much evidence that Koresh was a liar, a madman, a sadist or a combination of all three still believe he was the messiah? This can only be attributed to cognitive dissonance. They embraced a lie to avoid the pain that the truth would bring, and it cost them their lives and the lives of their children.

Are we proposing that a group of evangelicals will start teaching heretical doctrines, build a compound and become so paranoid that they kill federal agents who try to arrest them and commit mass suicide? It seems unlikely now, but it would not be impossible given a certain set of circumstances. What we wish to stress, though, is that the Waco incident is harsh modern-day proof that the doomsday mentality can have severe consequences for those who get caught up in it

Harold Camping

The most recent case of this phenomenon occurred just last year when Harold Camping's prediction that Christ would return between September 15 and 27, 1994, was proved incorrect. Camping, who owns a large network of Christian radio stations, announced his prediction in 1992. He proclaimed his views regularly on his nightly radio show and wrote two books on the subject, *1994?* and a sequel, *Are You Ready?* He offers the typical elaborate approach of most prognosticators: He twists Scripture to make his interpretations plausible, becomes preoccupied with elaborate biblical chronologies and tries to solve the complexities of biblical numerology through complicated and dubious calculations. For instance, Camping theorizes that May 1988 marked, precisely, the thirteen thousandth anniversary of the creation of the world. He determined that the end would come 2,300 days (Dan 8:14) later, or in September 1994.[71]

No one knows how many claim allegiance to Camping and his predictions, but his radio show is broadcast across the country on thirty-nine stations (and internationally on fourteen short-wave transmitters), and eighty thousand copies of his two books are in print. Following the profile of those susceptible to the doomsday mentality we established in the previous chapter, it is said that many who were attracted to Camping's predictions had become disillusioned with the current moral state of America. Camping's views have been challenged by several evangelicals, including two who publicly debated him for seven hours. At the end of that marathon, in which his theories came under exhaustive scrutiny, Camping commented, "If anything, I became more convicted than ever that we're headed right toward the end." Once again, we see that it is difficult to face reality when the doomsday mentality prevails. In fact, following the pattern of separation we discussed previously, Camping founded his own church, which boasted three hundred members before the September disappointment. Further, Camping's network, Family Radio, had a 15 to 20 percent increase in giving, to $12 million, as the deadline approached. Like the publishers of Whisenant's *88 Reasons*, Camping justified his prediction by stating that people were coming to Christ through the proclamation of his message.[72]

Given what we have learned so far, it is not surprising that as the September 27 deadline passed, Camping did not admit he was wrong. Following the Millerites' response to the Great Disappointment 150 years ago, Camping said he had simply miscalculated and firmly believed Christ would still come before 1994 ended. He viewed the delay in Christ's return as a time of testing to separate those who had truly converted from those whose commitment was shallow. The same held true for some of his followers. Kevin Brown, who hosted a Bible study in his home for Camping devotees, said in an interview with *Christianity Today,* "We still feel the Lord is going to come very soon, although it doesn't look very likely it will be in September. . . . This might be for [God's] glory. He might allow the world and church to revile us for a time. That might be part of his plan."[73] These words could have come from the mouth of any number of Millerites in October 1844. It seems once again that there is strong evidence to prove that people would rather rationalize something they know to be untrue than accept that the prediction they put their faith in was wrong.

Conclusion

This phenomenon—refusing to accept that Camping made a false prediction—is frightening because it did not occur a thousand years ago or a hundred years ago but so recently. Those who believe that none of what we have described here can happen to evangelicals today need only look to Harold Camping and his disciples. His following was not large, but under the certain conditions thousands—and perhaps millions, given the abilities of today's sophisticated broadcasting technology—could be led astray by someone like Camping.

In this chapter, we have tried to demonstrate the consequences of becoming obsessed with the Second Coming. We have looked at contemporary examples, but we focused on the Millerites not only because their circumstances so parallel our own, but also because they prove that a mass movement fixated on the Lord's return could easily form among mainstream, rational evangelicals. Millerism became a sectarian movement once its members viewed themselves as possessing some truth that all other Christians did not have and refused to accept. The mocking and criticism from secular and religious sources proved to them that they were a persecuted remnant that must remain faithful to what they thought was God's declaration: his son would return by 1844. All doctrines then became subordinate to the Second Coming. Once this separation took place, the Millerites opened themselves to bizarre and even heretical behavior.

So much of their hope was placed in the predictions for the Second Advent that when it did not come the Millerites were unable to cope with the shock. Most experienced painful despair from which they never quite recovered or joined groups that held to unorthodox doctrines. Others, because their commitment to the movement was so strong, refused to accept the fact that the predictions had failed. These Millerites seemed to experience more dire consequences than those who were able to face the truth. To suppress any doubts they may have had, they intensified their efforts to promote the movement, hoping that if people could still be converted to their beliefs, those beliefs must in some way be correct. They would then be vindicated. So, it is clear why they could not let go of their beliefs under any circumstances. Instead they heightened their efforts at proselytizing others, and even today several sects find their roots in William Miller's failed predictions, including David Koresh and the others who died in a blaze believing the false prophecy that they were being purified by God.

This process can be explained by the phenomenon known as cognitive dissonance. Some people become so committed to certain convictions, such as the return of Christ on a certain date, that they cannot discard them even when they are proved wrong. The emotional and psychological anguish that would accompany such an admission would be too much to bear. They avoid facing such pain by rationalizing the convictions proved untrue in such a way that they do indeed seem true. They may also intensify their efforts to win over more people—if they can convince others that their beliefs are right, then perhaps they indeed are right.

Some may argue that doctrinal positions do not affect average evangelicals in their daily walk with Christ. We have tried to show, however, that there are consequences to being obsessed with the Second Coming. The stage is set today for another Millerite-type movement in which the dynamics of cognitive dissonance may be displayed. People who believe they are living in the last generation before Christ's return and look to the year 2000 as a significant eschatological date will begin to interpret current events as if they were fulfillments of biblical prophecy. They may also be tempted to set dates for the Lord's return, as is already happening today, even though those who do it often refuse to admit it.

They may become isolated from a world that is becoming more corrupt and unpredictable. They may separate also from fellow Christians who have not seen the light of their narrowly defined eschatological positions. This isolation would become more pronounced as secular and Christian critics alike question the group's separation and exclusive views. All Christians hope for the imminent return of Christ, but to believe, without a doubt, that Christ is returning within months or even days would have a drastic effect on day-to-day life. Everything else would become minuscule compared to that expectation.

What would happen, then, if the Lord did not return when it was predicted that he would? Is it unreasonable to believe that these people would become disillusioned and abandon the faith or join heretical groups where they might find acceptance as the Millerites did? Is it unthinkable that others may not be able to cope with the fact that Christ did not return? They most likely would deny the truth of the situation and create scenarios for rationalizing the false prediction. This invariably would lead to serious heretical breaches from orthodoxy and intensified efforts to win people over to a false gospel.

We have focused on those who might get caught up in the doomsday mentality. We have not discussed the consequences such behavior might have on those outside such a movement. How might society at large react? Just a few years ago the entire nation of South Korea was overtaken by anxiety and panic when Lee Jang Kim predicted the rapture would occur in October 1992. While widespread fear may not occur if such an incident takes place in the United States, it goes without saying a Millerite-type movement would certainly tarnish the reputation of evangelicals, hinder the cause of Christ and damage the witness of Scripture. It is said that Millerism demolished premillennialism for years; we can only imagine what effect the movement had on the proclamation of the gospel. Our message is simply that if all of this happened in the past, it could happen again today.

Eschatology is exalted in our thinking and in our lives, as well it should be. We certainly do not wish to trivialize the doctrine or discourage those who correctly find comfort in the hope of Christ's return. Our only desire is to show how and under what conditions the truth could be misinterpreted and misused. What then is the proper role of eschatology in the Christian life? We offer a response in the conclusion.

Conclusion

Living in the Light of the Second Coming

WE WANT TO REAFFIRM HERE THAT OUR CRITIQUE OF THE doomsday mentality should not be misconstrued to mean that we disparage biblical prophecy. In fact, it is precisely because we are deeply committed to God's prophetic Word that we have written this book. That prophetic Word needs to be interpreted accurately; hence, the rationale behind our criticism of doomsayers.

Having said that, however, the question remains, How are we at the end of the twentieth century to respond properly to the imminent return of Christ? That the New Testament portrays the return of Christ as imminent (that is, it can happen at any time)[1] is clear and, we believe, proceeds from the early church's belief that the first coming of Christ inaugurated the signs of the times and the age to come. In other words, because the signs of the times were already set in motion in the first century A.D., the New Testament church focused its attention more on the *Son* than on the *signs*. What remained in history was but the coming intensification and culmination of those signs of the times that had already been initiated and thereby assured Christ's return. Thus, the early church seemed to view the Second Coming of Christ as an apt epilogue to his first coming.

An illustration made famous by Oscar Cullmann, the Swiss theologian of a generation ago, comes to mind. In his masterful book on New Testament eschatology, *Christ and Time,*[2] Cullmann compared the first and second comings of Christ to D-day and V-E Day of World War II. Just as D-day marked the beginning of the end for the Axis alliance armies, so the death and resurrection of Jesus signaled the victorious invasion of this age by the kingdom of God. Even after D-day, however, there was another year of war and death before the final victory. So, too, even after the triumph of Jesus' resurrection, spiritual warfare will continue to be the lot of God's people until the parousia. The outcome of that battle, however, is not in doubt; the Christian is on the victor's side.

What we are describing here is the theological mindset of the New Testament—the "already/not yet" end-time tension that exists between the first and second comings of Christ. And it is to the New Testament that we must ultimately look to answer the question of how we are to respond to the imminent return of Christ. In doing so, we believe five key responses of the first-century church emerge which serve as a model for Christians about to enter the twenty-first century.

First, in response to the imminent return of Christ, *the early church became heavily engaged in evangelism.* The two ideas, the Second Coming of Christ and evangelism, are complementary; after all, one of the signs of the times of Christ's return was his promise that "the gospel must first be preached to all nations" (Mk 13:10/Mt 24:14; compare Lk 21:12-15). Two texts in particular emphasize the early church's commitment to evangelism in light of the parousia. Like all the passages we will summarize here, these two texts display the already/not yet eschatological tension. Simply put, the church is to help convert sinners to the spiritual kingdom of God until the physical kingdom arrives.

The first passage we call attention to is the text of the Great

Commission in Matthew 28:18-20. According to these verses, the risen Jesus currently possesses all authority in heaven and on earth. This is nothing less than the inauguration of the messianic kingdom and the age to come (see also 1 Cor 15:20-28; Eph 1:18-23; Col 1:13-14), and it points to the "already" aspect of end-time prophecy. Because King Jesus reigns, sinners are to be converted into his kingdom, by faith. Nevertheless, that spiritual reign exists in the context of this present age, as indicated by the words at the end of the passage, "And surely I am with you always, to the very *end of the age*" (emphasis added). The continuance of the present age refers to the "not yet" aspect of end-time prophecy.

Acts 1:3-8 makes basically the same point. The "already" aspect of the kingdom of God is highlighted in verse 3. There Luke indicates that Jesus' resurrection was, in effect, the beginning of the dawning of the kingdom of God (compare 1 Cor 15:20-25). According to verses 4-5 and 8, the indwelling of God's people by the Holy Spirit (itself a sign of the arrival of the last days; see, for example, Joel 2:28-29 and Ezek 36:26-28) was confirmation that the kingdom of God has come. According to verses 6-7, however, the apostles mistook Jesus' words to mean that the physical kingdom, including the restoration of Israel, was at hand, a notion the Lord quickly corrected. This is the "not yet" aspect of end-time prophecy. Interestingly enough, the task to be discharged between Jesus' first and second comings is worldwide evangelization, through the power of the Spirit (v. 8).

Second, in looking for the return of Christ, *the early church committed itself to a holy lifestyle.* Many New Testament passages, of which Titus 2:11-14 is a good example, make the point that the proper response to the parousia is to live a godly life.

In Titus 2:12 Paul presents the two types of lifestyles that confront people in this present "age": ungodliness and righteousness. This tradition of the "two ways" is highlighted in the Old Testament (Gen 6:5; 8:21; Deut 8; Ps 1) and appropriated in the New Testament (Mt 7:24-29; Gal 5:16-26; Col 3:8-14; James 3:13-18). The assumption underlying this teaching is that the children of God will distinguish themselves as a holy people in the midst of this age, which is given over to sin.

According to Titus 2:11, 13-14, though, the age to come has broken into this present age through Jesus' death and resurrection. In other words, the age to come has already dawned, but it is not yet complete. The former aspect is attested to in verses 11 and 14, which speak of the appearing, or epiphany, of the grace of God through Christ's death, together with the salvation that he brought (v. 11), and of Christ giving himself for us that he might redeem us (v. 14). The latter aspect is emphasized to in verse 13, "We wait for the blessed hope—the glorious appearing [epiphany] of our great God and Savior, Jesus Christ."

The end-time tension that results from the first and second comings of Christ forms the basis for the ethical struggle between the two ways delineated in verse 12. Christians are called to declare their allegiance to the righteousness of the age to come instead of to the ungodliness that characterizes this age. That is, they must live like the people of the age to come while residing in the midst of this present evil age.³

Third, *the early church displayed an indomitable attitude in the midst of affliction, knowing that suffering produces eternal glory.* In fact, the early believers recognized that such heavenly glory had already dawned in their hearts by virtue of the resurrection of Jesus, but that their bodies would not be transformed until the parousia. Typical of this conviction are passages like Romans 8:17-25, 1 Peter 1:4-9 and Revelation 1:5-9. The attitude informing these passages, as we argued elsewhere, is rooted in the Jewish apocalyptic belief that righteous suffering in this age ensures heavenly glory in the age to come (see 4 Ezra 4:27; 7:12; *2 Apocalypse of Baruch* 15:8; 48:50; *The Damascus Rule* 3:18-20/4:13, 17-18).⁴

The Jewish perspective of the two ages, however, was consecutive in nature—when Messiah comes, this age will completely give way to the age to come. But according to the New Testament, those two ages now overlap because of the death and resurrection of Christ. Consequently, Christians, because they are in Jesus Messiah, currently and simultaneously participate in the sufferings of Christ's cross and in the glory of his resurrection. But at present this glory characterizes the believer's inner person; not until the parousia will it transform his or her body. This is the basic point made in Romans 8:17-25, 1 Peter 1:4-9 and Revelation 1:5-9.

It may even be that the New Testament understood these afflictions to be the long-awaited messianic woes that were expected to intensify and, like the pains of childbirth, give birth to the Messiah and his glorious reign on earth (see Dan 12:1; 4 Ezra 7:37; *2 Apocalypse of Baruch* 55:6). We previously noted that some authors make a rather convincing case for seeing Jesus' suffering on the cross as imprinted by this concept of the messianic woes. And, although Jesus has risen to glory, his followers live in between the two ages, hence their concomitant suffering and glory.[5] One day, however, affliction will completely give way to glory. Indeed, the very presence of such affliction assures the Christian of that future glory.

Fourth, in awaiting the return of Christ *the early church was not deceived by false teachers.* This discerning attitude was also informed by the already/not yet tension. On the one hand, the early church recognized that the spirit of antichrist had already dawned, especially in those who denied Jesus Christ (see 1 Jn 2:18-23; compare Jn 13:27; 2 Thess 2:1-12; 1 Tim 4:1-14; 2 Tim 4:1-5; 2 Pet 2:1-22; Jude 4-16; Rev 6—19). On the other hand, Jesus had earlier warned his disciples not to be tricked by such people into thinking that history was necessarily about to culminate (Mt 24:5-8). Luke 21:8-9 is interesting in this regard, for it makes the point that the spirit of antichrist (which basically amounted to people falsely claiming to be the Messiah) was only the *beginning* of the appearance of the signs of the times, not the end. Apparently we are to learn from this statement the fact that there were false teachers in the New Testament era claiming that the end of the world was near. Such people, say the Gospels, are to be avoided.

The church at the end of the twentieth century can profit from Jesus' warning not to assume that the presence of false teachers (the spirit of antichrist) inevitably signals the immediate revelation of the antichrist. Unfortunately, Christians have a long track record of identifying prominent individuals as the antichrist: several popes, Adolf Hitler, Benito Mussolini, John F. Kennedy, Henry Kissinger, Mikhail

Gorbachev and Juan Carlos. The same can be said of the enigmatic number 666, which has been equated with everything from credit cards to computers to the hand stamp at Disney World. The modern church needs to do away with such inappropriate speculation, which is informed by an anachronistic reading of current events back into the Bible. When the real antichrist is permitted by God to be revealed, no one will need to guess his identity, according to 2 Thessalonians 2:1-12. In the meantime, the believer is to be wary of, but not unduly alarmed by, false teachers, in regard to the return of Christ.

Fifth, in hoping for the parousia *the early church was encouraged in its struggle against Satan.* At the cross and resurrection of Christ the defeat of Satan and his demonic host was secured. At the Second Coming of Christ, their defeat will be sealed. A number of New Testament passages deal with this tension, including Colossians 2:15. This verse, along with 2:8, 20, is the classic Pauline text on the defeat of the anti-God spiritual rulers and authorities. Together they illustrate that the cross and resurrection of Christ are bringing about the demise of the evil powers, though their ultimate destruction is yet future. Thus verse 15 portrays the "already" side of the victory over the principalities, while verses 8 and 20 ("the elements of the world") present the "not yet" aspect (the demonic figures are still forces to be reckoned with.)

In verse 15, three graphic verbs are used to depict Christ's victory over the angelic powers: "stripped," "disgraced" and "triumphed over." The latter description is especially engaging because it calls to mind the ancient Roman triumphal procession, in which the victorious general marched proudly through the streets of Rome to celebrate his military accomplishments. Adam Clarke's description of that ancient custom accentuates the magnificence of Christ's victory over Satan and his demonic denizens:

He [the general] was carried in a magnificent chariot, adorned with ivory and plates of gold, and usually drawn by two white horses. Musicians led up the procession, and played triumphal pieces in praise of the general; and these were followed by young men, who led the victims which were to be sacrificed on the occasion, with

154 _____ DOOMSDAY DELUSIONS

their horns gilded, and their heads and necks adorned with ribbons and garlands. Next followed carts loaded with the spoils taken from the enemy, with their horses and chariots. These were followed by the kings, princes, or generals taken in the war, loaded with chains. Immediately after these came the triumphal chariot, before which, as it passed, the people strewed flowers and shouted, "Io, triumphe!" The triumphal chariot was followed by the senate; and the procession was closed by the priests and the attendants, with the different sacrificial utensils, and a white ox, which was to be the chief victim. They then passed through the triumphal arch, along the via sacra to the capital, where the victims were slain. During this time all the temples were opened, and every altar smoked with offerings and incense.[7]

That these spiritual powers have not yet been annihilated, or even domesticated, however, is clear from verses 8 and 20, for there Paul challenges the Colossian Christians not to permit themselves to be enslaved to "the principles of this world," which undoubtedly involve hostile angelic beings.[8] Rather, they need to reaffirm the defeat of the supernatural powers by continually submitting themselves to the lordship of Christ. Such an admonition assumes the "not yet" aspect of Paul's perspective on the Christian life.[9]

While there may be more responses of the New Testament church to the imminent return of Christ that could be identified, these five should sufficiently occupy Christians of all times until that event transpires. We wish to conclude our comments on the subject with Paul's word in 1 Thessalonians 4:18. After describing the return of the Lord, the apostle writes, "Therefore encourage each other with these words." We have shown that biblical prophecy can be misused in a number of ways. Some treat it like a toy, playing with prophetic symbols and numbers. Others use prophecy as if it were a weapon, fighting anyone who does not see future things quite the way they do. According to Paul, however, the purpose of biblical prophecy is to comfort and encourage believers. We are confident that Christ will come again to right all the injustices we see in the world and to take us home to be with him forever. We cannot know the exact time of

Christ's return, but we must live as if it could happen at any moment. It is this message that empowers Christians to live in the light of the Second Coming every day of their lives.

Notes

Preface

[1]Sam Howe Verhovek, "Scores Die As Cult Compound Is Set Afire After F.B.I. Sends in Tanks with Tear Gas: Apparent Mass Suicide Ends a 51-Day Standoff in Texas," *New York Times,* April 20, 1993, pp. A1, A12; Nancy Gibbs, " 'Oh, My God, They're Killing Themselves!' " *Time,* May 3, 1993, pp. 26-43.

[2]Verhovek, "Scores Die As Cult Compound Is Set Afire," pp. A1, A12; Kenneth Samples, Erwin de Castro, Richard Abanes and Robert Lyle, *Prophets of the Apocalypse: David Koresh and Other American Messiahs* (Grand Rapids, Mich.: Baker, 1994), p. 78.

[3]Samples et al., *Prophets of the Apocalypse,* pp. 77-96.

[4]Richard Lacayo, "Heading for the Hills," *Time,* March 26, 1990, p. 20; "Sect Ordered to Stop Work on Bomb Shelters," *Los Angeles Times,* April 24, 1990, p. A18.

[5]Teresa Watanabe, "No Doomsday Rapture for S. Korea Sect," *Los Angeles Times,* October 29, 1992, p. A1; "Life as Usual Brings Anger," *Chicago Tribune,* October 29, 1992, evening update edition, p. 1.

[6]David Briggs, Associated Press wire service story, July 13, 1994, n.p.; Joe Maxwell, "End-times Prediction Draws Strong Following," *Christianity Today,* June 20, 1994, pp. 46-47; Joe Maxwell, "Camping Misses End-times Deadline," *Christianity Today,* October 24, 1994, p. 84.

[7]Alan Riding, "48 from Sect Dead After Mass Ritual in Switzerland: 2 Found Dead in Canada—Fear More," *New York Times,* October 6, 1994, pp. A1, A8; William Drozdiak, "48 Cult Followers Found Shot, Burned in Swiss Villages: Collective Suicide Suspected in Booby-Trapped Buildings," *Washington Post,* October 6, 1994, p. A1; Michael S. Serrill, "Remains of the Day," *Time,* October 24, 1994, p. 42.

[8]Nicholas D. Kristof, "Hundreds in Japan Hunt Gas Attackers After 8 Die: Police Tighten Security Steps at Stations," *New York Times,* March 21, 1995, pp. A1, A6; Sheryl Wu Dunn, "Japanese Cult: A Strong Lure and a Danger to Challenge," *New*

York Times, March 24, 1995, pp. A1, A4; David Van Biema, "Prophet of Poison," *Time,* April 3, 1995, pp. 28-32. James Walsh, "Shoko Asahara: The Making of a Messiah," *Time,* April 3, 1995, pp. 30-31.

Chapter 1: When Prophecy Fails

[1]Dwight Wilson makes this connection between the "Shepherd Boy and the Wolf" and doomsday preachers in *Armageddon Now! The Premillenarian Response to Russia and Israel Since 1917* (Grand Rapids, Mich.: Baker, 1977), p. vii.

[2]In a *U.S. News & World Report* survey, 61 percent of those responding said they believe "Jesus Christ will return to Earth" (Jeffery L. Sheler, "The Christmas Covenant," *U.S. News & World Report,* December 19, 1994, p. 62).

[3]Paul Boyer, *When Time Shall Be No More: Prophecy Beliefs in Modern American Culture* (Cambridge, Mass.: Harvard University Press, 1992), pp. 2-3. Other authors who provide a scholarly critique of modern doomsday prophecy include: Michael J. St. Clair, *Millenarian Movements in Historical Context* (New York: Garland, 1992); Daniel Cohen, *Waiting for the Apocalypse* (Buffalo, N.Y.: Prometheus, 1973); Timothy P. Weber, *Living in the Shadow of the Second Coming: American Premillenialism 1875-1925* (New York: Oxford University Press, 1979); Ernest R. Sandeen, *The Roots of Fundamentalism: British and American Millenarianism 1800-1930* (Chicago: University of Chicago Press, 1970).

[4]Modern-day apocalyptic seers include: Grant R. Jeffrey, *Armageddon: Appointment with Destiny* (Toronto: Frontier Research, 1988); Chuck Smith, *Future Survival* (Costa Mesa, Calif.: Calvary Chapel, 1978); Edgar C. Whisenant, *88 Reasons Why the Rapture Will Be in 1988* (Nashville: World Bible Society, 1988); Wesley Meacham, *Troubled Waters: Prophecy from a Layman's Point of View* (New York: Vantage, 1988); David Reagan, *The Master Plan: Making Sense of the Controversies Surrounding Bible Prophecy Today* (Eugene, Ore.: Harvest House, 1993).

[5]Reagan, *The Master Plan,* p. 210.

[6]Meacham, *Troubled Waters,* p. 37.

[7]Reagan, *The Master Plan,* p. 5.

[8]D. S. Russell, *Apocalyptic: Ancient and Modern* (Philadelphia: Fortress, 1978), p. 64.

[9]David E. Aune, *Prophecy in Early Christianity and the Ancient Mediterranean World* (Grand Rapids, Mich.: Eerdmans, 1983), pp. 188-89. Josephus recounts a similar incident with regard to an unnamed Egyptian Jew (*Antiquities of the Jews* 20.169-172; *Jewish Wars* 2.261-63); compare Acts 21:38.

[10]Russell Chandler, *Doomsday: The End of the World. A View Through Time* (Ann Arbor, Mich.: Servant Publications, 1993), pp. 47-48.

[11]For Miller's actual calculations, see Timothy J. Chandler, "Miller and the Millennium: William Miller as Part of the Nineteenth-Century Millennialist Movement" (paper delivered in the American Studies Department, Willamette University,

Salem, Oregon, 1990), pp. 9-12; quoted in Russell Chandler, *Doomsday,* p. 185.

[12]Whisenant, *88 Reasons.*

[13]Edgar C. Whisenant, *The Final Shout: Rapture Report 1989, 1990, 1991, 1992, 1993 . . .* (Nashville: World Bible Society, 1989).

[14]For example, one can imagine that the doomsday prophets saw the 1993 peace pact between Israel and the PLO as the beginning of the seven-year peace in the Middle East prophesied in Daniel 9:24-27. In fact, evangelist Jack van Impe claimed as much on his January 2, 1994, TV program. In chapter three of this book we will challenge that interpretation.

[15]George Ladd was the first to propose this nomenclature, in "Why Not Prophetic-Apocalyptic?" *Journal of Biblical Literature* 76 (1957): 192-200.

[16]The term is Aune's in *Prophecy in Early Christianity,* which provides an excellent discussion of the genre, pp. 121-37.

[17]D. S. Russell, *The Method and Message of Jewish Apocalyptic* (Philadelphia: Westminster, 1964), pp. 37-38, whose work is the classic analysis of the subject.

[18]Ibid., p. 39.

[19]Leon Morris, *Apocalyptic* (Grand Rapids, Mich.: Eerdmans, 1972), pp. 34-61. The literature on apocalypticism is extensive. For a good bibliography of the more recent works, see Alan F. Johnson, "Revelation," in *Hebrews—Revelation,* ed. Frank E. Gaebelein, vol. 12 of Expositor's Bible Commentary (Grand Rapids, Mich.: Zondervan, 1981), p. 400, n. 3.

[20]George Ladd, "Apocalyptic," in *Baker's Dictionary of Theology,* ed. E. F. Harrison (Grand Rapids, Mich.: Baker, 1960).

[21]Though evangelicals would have a problem with applying items 1, 7 and 8 to biblical books.

[22]J. Barton Payne, *Encyclopedia of Biblical Prophecy* (New York: Harper & Row, 1973), pp. 86-87.

[23]Henry Virkler, *Hermeneutics: Principles and Processes of Biblical Interpretation* (Grand Rapids, Mich.: Baker, 1988), pp. 95-112.

[24]C. H. Dodd, *The Apostolic Preaching and Its Developments* (New York: Harper, 1944), pp. 38-45.

[25]Gordon D. Fee, *1 and 2 Timothy, Titus* (Peabody, Mass.: Hendrickson, 1988), p. 19.

[26]C. E. B. Cranfield, *Romans IX—XVI,* International Critical Commentary (Edinburgh: T. & T. Clark, 1979), p. 683.

[27]Harold Camping, *Are You Ready?* (New York: Vantage, 1993), p. 3.

[28]Grant R. Jeffrey, *Armageddon: Appointment with Destiny* (Toronto: Frontier Research, 1988), p. 193.

[29]Smith, *Future Survival,* p. 20.

[30]Salem Kirban, *Countdown to Rapture* (Eugene, Ore.: Harvest House, 1977), p. 14.

[31]Quoted in Chandler, *Doomsday,* p. 257, though Robertson later acknowledged he had gone too far in his prediction.

[32]Charles R. Taylor is well known through his *Bible Prophecy News* and radio program, "Today in Bible Prophecy."

[33]James McKeever publishes his *End-Times News Digest,* Medford, Oregon. Compare Dave Hunt and his publication, *Berean Call,* Bend, Oregon.

[34]Mary Stewart Relfe, *When Your Money Fails: The 666 System Is Here* (Montgomery, Ala.: Ministries, 1981).

[35]Wim Malgo, *There Shall Be Signs in Heaven and on Earth* (Columbia, S.C.: Midnight Call, 1980).

Chapter 2: The Signs of the Times

[1]"Interview: Tony Campolo," *The Door,* September/October 1993, p. 14.

[2]Classical dispensationalism was popularized by the Scofield Bible, which has enjoyed enormous popularity in America during the twentieth century. Its ablest defender is Charles Ryrie, *Dispensationalism Today* (Chicago: Moody Press, 1965). Ryrie, like many classical dispensationalists, argues that God's dealings with humanity can be categorized into various dispensations, or periods of time (innocence, conscience, civil government, promise, law, grace, tribulation and millennium). Each time frame consists of three parts: (1) divine revelation; (2) human disobedience; (3) a new dispensation, thanks to God's mercy. According to Ryrie, there are three hallmarks of classical dispensationalism: (1) it interprets prophetic Scriptures literally; (2) it separates the promises to Israel from those to the church; (3) the purpose of the Bible is to highlight the glory of God. Ryrie makes these points vis-à-vis Reformed theology, or covenantalism. The latter sees basically one dispensation or covenant in the Bible—grace through faith. Furthermore, covenantalism is said to differ with the three hallmarks of dispensationalism: (1) it holds to a symbolic interpretation of prophetic Scriptures; (2) it views the church as the permanent replacement of Israel (and hence there is no future for national Israel); (3) the purpose of the Bible is to unfold the story of the salvation of humans. As so often is the case in theological debate, however, adherents of these views seem to have overstated their disagreements to the exclusion of the many points they share in common. We feel comfortable classifying ourselves in the dispensational camp, or at least in a revised form of it. Actually, our work attempts to make the point that dispensationalism need not lead to a doomsday prophetic approach.

[3]Progressive dispensationalists wish to modify the claims of classical dispensationalism by conceding a number of points to their covenantalist brethren: (1) apocalyptic and prophetic Scriptures are to be interpreted in a symbolic way, behind which lies the literal reality; (2) salvation in the Old Testament was based on grace through faith; (3) the kingdom of God dawned in the ministry of Jesus and continues today in spiritual form. Covenantalists, for their part, show signs of conceding to their dispensationalist brethren the point that God still has a place for Israel and will one day restore its land. For an example of the rapprochement between the two

traditions, see John S. Feinberg, ed., *Continuity and Discontinuity: Perspectives on the Relationship Between the Old and New Testaments. Essays in Honor of S. Lewis Johnson, Jr.,* (Wheaton, Ill.: Crossway Books, 1988).

[4]The following discussion of the day of the Lord comes from C. Marvin Pate, *The End of the Age Has Come: The Theology of Paul* (Grand Rapids, Mich.: Zondervan/Harper and Collins, 1995), chap. 9.

[5]Joseph A. Fitzmyer, *The Gospel According to Luke X—XXIV,* Anchor Bible, 28A (New York: Doubleday, 1983), p. 1329.

[6]See the works by J. Massyngberde Ford, *Revelation,* Anchor Bible, 38 (New York: Doubleday, 1975), especially her exposition of Revelation 6 and 17; Alan James Beagley, *The "Sitz im Leben" of the Apocalypse with Particular Reference to the Role of the Church's Enemies* (New York: Walter de Gruyter, 1987), especially chap. 2; Kenneth L. Gentry Jr., *Before Jerusalem Fell: Dating the Book of Revelation* (Tyler, Tex.: Institute for Christian Economics, 1989).

[7]R. H. Charles, *A Critical and Exegetical Commentary on the Revelation of St. John,* 2 vols., International Critical Commentary (Edinburgh: T. & T. Clark, 1920), 1:158; compare Louis A. Vos, *The Synoptic Traditions in the Apocalypse* (Kampen, The Netherlands: Kok, 1965), pp. 181-92.

[8]The following discussion draws on Pate, *The End of the Age Has Come,* chap. 9.

[9]Hermann Gunkel, *Schöpfung und Chaos in Urzeit und Endzeit* (Göttingen: Vandenhoeck und Ruprecht, 1895), pp. 41-69.

[10]H. H. Rowley, *The Relevance of Apocalyptic: A Study of Jewish and Christian Apocalypses from Daniel to the Revelation* (London: Lutterworth, 1947), p. 46.

[11]For the identification of the restrainer as Michael the archangel, see C. Marvin Pate, *The Glory of Adam and the Afflictions of the Righteous: Pauline Suffering in Context* (Lewiston, N.Y.: Edwin Mellen, 1993), pp. 307-9.

[12]Massyngberde Ford delineates four major views regarding the identification of the first horseman: (1) the antichrist, (2) the Christ, (3) the historical events of the first century A.D. and (4) the angel of the Lord (Massyngberde Ford's view), *Revelation,* pp. 105-6. For a convincing defense of the first approach, that the rider on the white horse is antichrist or the false messiah, see Vos, *The Synoptic Traditions in the Apocalypse,* pp. 187-92.

[13]See the discussion by Massyngberde Ford, *Revelation,* pp. 106-7.

[14]For a summary of the atrocities of the Neronian era, see Kenneth L. Gentry, *The Beast of Revelation* (Tyler, Tex.: Institute for Christian Economics, 1989), pp. 40-46.

[15]Massyngberde Ford provides a thorough discussion of the debate as to whether one should begin with Julius Caesar (47-44 B.C.) or Caesar Augustus (31 B.C.-A.D. 14), as well as related matters on the identification of the ten kings, *Revelation,* pp. 210-17, 289-93.

[16]See Gentry's convenient summary of the issue, *The Beast of Revelation,* chap. 3.

[17]R. H. Charles, *The Revelation of John,* 2:69-70.

[18]So, for example, according to Massyngberde Ford, *Revelation*, pp. 285-88; Beagley, *The "Sitz im Leben" of the Apocalypse*, pp. 92-102.

[19]See Everett Ferguson's discussion of this topic, *Backgrounds of Early Christianity* (Grand Rapids, Mich.: Eerdmans, 1987), pp. 342-43.

[20]Note the comments by Austin Marsden Farrer, *The Revelation of St. John the Divine: Commentary on the English Text* (New York: Oxford University Press, 1964), p. 72. A rather clear indication that Jewish synagogues expelled Jewish Christians from their midst can be found in Benediction 12, "For the renegades let there be no hope, and may the arrogant kingdom soon be rooted out in our days, and the Nazarenes and the *minîm* ["heretics"] perish as in a moment and be blotted out from the book of life and with the righteous may they not be inscribed. Blessed art thou, O Lord, who humblest the arrogant" (quoted in C. K. Barrett, *The New Testament Background: Selected Documents* [New York: Harper & Row, 1961], p. 167). The Nazarenes are the *minîm* ("heretics") and are most probably to be identified as Jewish Christians.

[21]See Gentry, *The Beast of Revelation*, pp. 71-75; Robert H. Mounce, *The Book of Revelation*, New International Commentary (Grand Rapids, Mich.: Eerdmans, 1977), p. 253.

[22]Chandler presents the scientific evidence suggesting that it is not earthquakes that are on the increase but rather that modern devices are better at detecting tremors than they were in the past (Russell Chandler, *Doomsday: The End of the World—A View Through Time* [Ann Arbor, Mich.: Servant Publications, 1993], pp. 138-40).

[23]For the viewpoint that the earthquake referred to in Revelation 11:13 occurred in Jerusalem in A.D. 70, see Beagley, *The "Sitz im Leben" of the Apocalypse*, pp. 68-69.

[24]One has to also reckon with the possibility that Revelation 11:13 draws on Ezekiel 38:19.

[25]Dale C. Allison, *The End of the Ages Has Come: An Early Interpretation of the Passion and Resurrection of Jesus* (Philadelphia: Fortress, 1985), pp. 40-47.

[26]Ibid., p. 48.

[27]Eduard Schweizer, *The Good News According to Matthew*, trans. David E. Green (Atlanta: John Knox, 1975), p. 524; compare Allison, *The End of the Ages Has Come*, p. 48.

[28]This is a better referent than to Emperor Domitian's order in A.D. 92 prohibiting the planting of further vineyards in Italy and ordering the destruction of half the vineyards in other parts of the Roman Empire. Though often appealed to as the background of Revelation 6:6, the Domitian order is actually the opposite of that statement. Nor does the Domitian order explain the Apocalypse's reference to sparing the oil.

[29]Beagley discusses the possible interplay of events surrounding the fall of Jerusalem in A.D. 70 with Old Testament passages proclaiming divine judgment upon Jerusalem in determining the background of the fourth seal judgment of Revelation 6:7-8,

162 NOTES FOR PAGES 49-60

The "Sitz im Leben" of the Apocalypse, pp. 40-43.

[30]Allison, *The End of the Ages Has Come;* compare Pate, *The Glory of Adam.*

[31]Beagley, *The "Sitz im Leben" of the Apocalypse,* p. 36.

[32]Ibid., pp. 33-36, 84-90.

[33]Philip Carrington, *The Meaning of the Revelation* (London: SPCK, 1931), pp. 131-32. However, this type of comment should not be misconstrued as anti-Semitic. After all, the early Christians, John included, were Jewish. Moreover there are indications elsewhere in the New Testament that God will one day restore the people of Israel to himself and to their land (see Rom 11:25-27).

[34]The following discussion comes from Pate, *The End of the Age Has Come,* chap. 9.

[35]Allison, *The End of the Ages Has Come,* pp. 54-55.

[36]C. K. Barrett, *The Gospel According to John,* 2nd ed. (Philadelphia: Westminster, 1978), p. 58.

[37]Wendy E. Sproston, "Satan in the Fourth Gospel," in *Studia Biblica 1978. II. Papers on the Gospels, Journal for the Study of the New Testament* Supplement Series 2, ed. E. A. Livingstone (Sheffield: JSOT, 1980), pp. 308-9.

[38]Ferguson, *Backgrounds of Early Christianity,* pp. 342-43.

[39]Beagley, *The "Sitz im Leben" of the Apocalypse,* pp. 44-45.

[40]See Pate, *The End of the Age Has Come,* chap. 9.

Chapter 3: This Generation Will Not Pass Away

[1]Robert B. Chisholm Jr., "Evidence from Genesis," in *A Case for Premillennialism: A New Consensus,* ed. Donal K. Campbell and Jeffrey L. Townsend (Chicago: Moody Press, 1992), p. 35; see pp. 35-54. *Premillennial* means that Christ will return before the millennium, at which time he will set up his thousand-year reign on earth. *Amillennial* means that there will not be a literal thousand-year reign of Christ on earth, but rather that he reigns now from heaven through the church. *Postmillennial* means that Christ will return after a thousand-year utopia on earth. Chisholm includes a sample bibliography representing the various views (p. 35).

[2]Chisholm provides a masterful and convincing defense of the unconditionality of the Abrahamic covenant, "Evidence from Genesis," pp. 35-54. As further proof that the Abrahamic covenant is unconditional, it is important to note the "jeopardy principle" in Genesis. That is, even though Abraham sinned on at least three occasions, thus jeopardizing God's covenant with him, nevertheless in each case God overruled Abraham's failure and maintained his covenant with the patriarch (Gen 12—Abraham lied about Sarah to Pharaoh; Gen 16—Abraham had the child Ishmael by Sarah's handmaid Hagar; Gen 20—Abraham lied to Abimelech).

[3]Many scholars identify the borders of ancient Israel in this way: the western border—the Mediterranean Sea; the southern border—the River of Egypt, which is Wadi-el-Arish (*not* the Nile River); the eastern border—the Arnon River in the Wilderness of Kedemoth; the northern border—the northern Euphrates River,

probably up to the great bend, Tiphsah (see Gen 15:18; Deut 11:24; 1 Kings 4:21, 24; 2 Chron 9:26; compare Judg 20:1; 1 Sam 3:20). For a careful discussion of the issue, see Barry J. Beitzel, *The Moody Atlas of Bible Lands* (Chicago: Moody Press, 1985), pp. 8-13.

[4]Chisholm, "Evidence from Genesis," p. 54.

[5]Typical of this identification is the work by Wim Malgo, *Israel's God Does Not Lie* (Hamilton, Ohio.: Midnight Call, 1974), pp. 90-91.

[6]For example, Beitzel observes that the Bible labels the following ancient enemies of Israel as from the North, even though they were located in the East: Assyrians (e.g., Zeph 2:13), Babylonians (e.g., Jer 1:13-15; 6:22; Zech 2:6-7), Persians (e.g., Is 41:25; Jer 50:3) *[The Moody Atlas of Bible Lands,* p. 4].

[7]Ibid., p. 5.

[8]Edwin Yamauchi, *Foes from the Northern Frontier* (Grand Rapids, Mich.: Baker, 1982), pp. 19-27; p. 20.

[9]Yamauchi, "A Russian Invasion of Iran," pp. 22-24. Perhaps the leading theory is that *Gog* referred to the famous king of Lydia, "Gyges," and that *Magog* referred to the "land of Gyges"; but there is no consensus among scholars about this identification. See Yamauchi, *Foes from the Northern Frontier,* p. 19-28.

[10]See Yamauchi on this identification, "A Russian Invasion of Iran," pp. 24-27. The testimony consists of the Assyrian texts (Tiglath-Pileser I [1115-1077 B.C.], Ashurnasirpal II [883-859 B.C.], Sargon II [721-705 B.C.], Herodotus [c. fourth century B.C., 7.72]; Josephus [c. A.D. 90, *Antiquities of the Jews* 1.124]).

[11]One should not overlook in this regard the possibility that Ezekiel applied the terminology of Gog and Magog to the fall of Jerusalem to the Babylonians in 587 B.C., which might foreshadow an end-time invasion of Israel. This would not be unlike the pattern we earlier detected in the Olivet Discourse concerning the fall of Jerusalem to the Romans in A.D. 70 representing a future end-time attack on Israel.

[12]Malgo, *Israel's God Does Not Lie,* pp. 91-93.

[13]We date the book of Daniel to the sixth century B.C., during the Babylonian exile, not, as others do, to the second century B.C., during the Maccabean revolt.

[14]This second view is often branded the "liberal" approach. However, R. Gurney has recently offered an evangelical rendition of this approach, except that he differs from the liberal approach in two significant ways (with which we agree): First, Gurney defends a sixth-century B.C. date for the book of Daniel and hence accepts the prophecies therein as predictions that were supernaturally fulfilled at a later time (and not as mere *vaticinia ex eventu*—pronouncements after the events). John H. Walton discusses a second reason that distinguishes Gurney's approach from the liberal interpretation:

> Another reason why the Greek hypothesis has been considered problematic by most conservative interpreters is that if Greece is the fourth empire, then Media is the second empire. This Median empire has been presented by critical scholars

as an historical misperception on the part of the author of Daniel. They view the empire as connected with Darius the Mede, whom they consider fictional. Gurney likewise avoids pitfalls here by suggesting that the Median empire that ought to be identified as the second kingdom is not a nonexistent realm ruled by a fictional Darius the Mede. Rather, it is the historically known Median empire that is contemporary to the Neo-Babylonian empire. His contention is that after the death of Nebuchadnezzar the Medes were actually more powerful than the declining Neo-Babylonian kings. ("The Four Kingdoms of Daniel 2 and 7," *Themelios* 2 [1977]: 39-45; compare John H. Walton's article, "The Four Kingdoms of Daniel," *Journal of the Evangelical Theological Society* 29, no. 1 [March 1986]: 25-36; p. 29.)

[15]See, for example, the discussion by André Lacocque, *The Book of Daniel,* trans. David Pellauer (Atlanta: John Knox, 1979), p. 139.

[16]Gurney, "The Four Kingdoms of Daniel 2 and 7," p. 43; Walton, "The Four Kingdoms of Daniel," pp. 30-31. Liberals also identify the second kingdom with the Median empire but discard the historicity of the biblical statement about its greatness. However, Walton ably defends the historical reliability of the biblical description.

[17]See the documentation of Gurney, "The Four Kingdoms of Daniel 2 and 7," p. 43, and Walton, "The Four Kingdoms of Daniel," p. 30.

[18]Walton, "The Four Kingdoms of Daniel," p. 30.

[19]Gurney, "The Four Kingdoms of Daniel 2 and 7," p. 43.

[20]Ibid., p. 43.

[21]Ibid., p. 44.

[22]See the thorough review of the history of the interpretation of Daniel 2 and 7 with special reference to the identification of the fourth kingdom by H. H. Rowley, *Darius the Mede and the Four World Empires in the Book of Daniel* (Cardiff: University of Wales, 1959).

[23]Gurney makes this point, "The Four Kingdoms of Daniel 2 and 7," p. 44. He also rightly adds that the fourth empire is said to crush the other three empires. While Greece did conquer all of the other three, Babylon, Media and Persia were all outside the Roman Empire.

[24]Ibid.

[25]Lacocque provides a good description of this situation (*The Book of Daniel,* p. 52). It may be that Daniel 2:43 refers to the failed marriage between Cleopatra, the daughter of Antiochus III, and Ptolemy V. Comparing Daniel 2 and 7 with chapter 8 yields the following historical development of ancient Greece, the fourth kingdom: Alexander the Great, the four kingdoms led by Alexander's four generals, two of which competed against each other for control—the Seleucids and the Ptolemies.

[26]Walton, "The Four Kingdoms of Daniel," p. 32.

[27]Ibid., pp. 33-34. We should note in passing that the identification of the kingdom of

God, described in Daniel 2:44 and 7:13, is disputed. Walton's treatment of this issue deserves quoting:

> The exact timing between the fourth kingdom and the kingdom of God is not clear in the text. Dan 7:11 has the fourth beast (including, presumably, the little horn) slain, then the Son of Man comes forward (7:13). No further explanation comes in 7:22-27. Dan 2:44, however, has been used to suggest that the kingdom of God must be set up "in the days of" the ten kings. If this is required by the text, then the hypothesis that I am considering here would fall short. It should be noted, however, that nowhere in chap. 2 of Daniel is there mention of a ten-kingdom stage. The toes are mentioned as being of iron and pottery along with the feet, but no symbolic value is given to the toes. The kings spoken of in 2:44 would be the kings of the kingdoms of this world (notice "all these kingdoms" toward the end of the verse). No definite chronological information is given. (p. 35, footnote 47.)

[28]J. A. Montgomery, *A Critical and Exegetical Commentary on the Book of Daniel* (Edinburgh: T. & T. Clark, 1927) p. 400.

[29]Michael Kalafian, *The Prophecy of the Seventy Weeks of the Book of Daniel* (Lanham, Md.: University Press of America, 1991). We earlier defined the premillennial and amillennial views (see footnote 1 of this chapter). The liberal view treats all Danielic prophecies as *vaticinia ex eventu* (pronouncements after the fact), not as legitimate predictions later supernaturally fulfilled in history.

[30]This is the famous calculation of Sir Robert Anderson in his book *The Coming Prince,* 14th ed. (Grand Rapids, Mich.: Kregel, 1954). Most scholars today correctly dismiss Anderson's ingenious interpretation as an artificial attempt to get Daniel's prophecy fulfilled by the first coming of Christ.

[31]John Goldingay, *Daniel,* Word Biblical Commentary, vol. 30 (Waco, Tex.: Word, 1989), p. 260.

[32]See Lacocque's defense of this calculation, *The Book of Daniel,* p. 178.

[33]Hal Lindsey, *The Late Great Planet Earth* (Grand Rapids, Mich.: Zondervan, 1969), p. 48.

[34]A. L. Moore, *The Parousia in the New Testament,* Supplement to *Novum Testamentum,* 13 (Leiden: E. J. Brill, 1966), pp. 132-36.

[35]Ibid., pp. 132-33.

[36]Ibid., p. 134.

[37]Ibid., pp. 134-35.

Chapter 4: The Separation of the Saints

[1]See, for instance, the following examples as recent expressions of this phenomenon: William J. Bennett, *The De-Valuing of America: The Fight for Our Culture and Our Children* (New York: Summit Books, 1992); Stephen L. Carter, *The Culture of Disbelief: How American Law and Politics Trivialize Religious Devotion* (New

York: Basic Books, 1993); Charles Dyer, *World News and Bible Prophecy* (Wheaton, Ill.: Tyndale House, 1995); Mark Hitchcock, *After the Empire: Bible Prophecy in Light of the Fall of the Soviet Union* (Wheaton, Ill.: Tyndale House, 1994); Dave Hunt, *Global Peace and the Rise of Antichrist* (Eugene, Ore.: Harvest House, 1990); James Davison Hunter, *Culture Wars: The Struggle to Define America* (New York: Basic Books, 1991); James Davison Hunter, *Before the Shooting Begins: Searching for Democracy in America's Culture War* (New York: Free Press, 1994); D. James Kennedy with Jim Nelson Black, *Character and Destiny: A Nation in Search of Its Soul* (Grand Rapids, Mich.: Zondervan, 1994); Tim and Beverly LaHaye, *A Nation Without a Conscience: Where Have All the Values Gone?* (Wheaton, Ill.: Tyndale House, 1994); Hal Lindsey, *Planet Earth—2000 A.D.: Will Mankind Survive?* (Palos Verdes, Calif.: Western Front, 1994); John F. MacArthur Jr., *The Vanishing Conscience: Drawing the Line in a No-Fault, Guilt-Free World* (Dallas, Tex.: Word, 1994); Pat Robertson, *The New World Order* (Dallas, Tex.: Word, 1992).

[2]For an excellent summary of how many people, especially evangelicals, have become obsessed with the coming of the new millennium, see Russell Chandler, *Doomsday: The End of the World—A View Through Time* (Ann Arbor, Mich.: Servant Publications), pp. 275-85.

[3]In the history of the church three major interpretations of the millennium have emerged: (1) Postmillennialists hold that the world will get better and better as the gospel is preached universally. When the world is evangelized, there will follow a wonderful extended period of peace and harmony, which is interpreted as the millennium. Christ will return after that euphoric time. (2) Amillennialists believe that the thousand years from which we get the term *millennium* are to be taken figuratively, as a spiritual reign of Christ, not literally, as a physical reign. The millennium then refers to the period between the first and second comings of Christ in which he rules spiritually in the lives of his followers. (3) Premillennialists take the millennium literally. They believe Christ will return physically to earth and actually rule for one thousand years from Jerusalem.

[4]For various views of the Bible conference movement in particular and fundamentalism in general, see the following: Stewart G. Cole, *The History of Fundamentalism* (Westport, Conn.: Greenwood, 1931); George M. Marsden, *Fundamentalism and American Culture: The Shaping of Twentieth-Century Evangelicalism, 1870-1925* (Oxford: Oxford University Press, 1980); George M. Marsden, *Understanding Fundamentalism and Evangelicalism* (Grand Rapids, Mich.: Eerdmans, 1991); Ernest R. Sandeen, *The Roots of Fundamentalism: British and American Millenarianism, 1800-1930* (Chicago: University of Chicago Press, 1970).

[5]Lindsey, *Planet Earth—2000 A.D.*, p. 289.

[6]*Midnight Cry,* March 10, 1843, n.p., quoted in Michael Barkun, *Crucible of the Millennium: The Burned-over District of New York in the 1840s* (Syracuse, N.Y.: Syracuse University Press, 1986), p. 56.

[7]B. J. Oropeza, *99 Reasons Why No One Knows When Christ Will Return* (Downers Grove, Ill.: InterVarsity Press, 1994), pp. 72-112.

[8]For a fascinating discussion of how the extent of media coverage around the world is greatly affecting the formation and execution of public policy, see James F. Hoge Jr., "Media Pervasiveness," *Foreign Affairs,* July/August 1994, pp. 136-44.

[9]Two good examples of this more optimistic perspective are found in Michael S. Horton, *Beyond Culture Wars: Is America a Mission Field or a Battle Field?* (Chicago: Moody Press, 1994) and Alister McGrath, *Evangelicalism and the Future of Christianity* (Downers Grove, Ill.: InterVarsity Press, 1995).

[10]"On to the Millennium," *Newsweek,* Dec. 26, 1994/Jan. 2. 1995, pp. 106-34. For a discussion of the hope that lies within the difficult challenges facing the church, see Russell Chandler, *Racing Toward 2001: The Forces Shaping America's Religious Future* (Grand Rapids, Mich.: Zondervan, 1992).

[11]Much of the following discussion loosely follows the theories on sects and millenarianism developed in the field of the sociology of religion. For an excellent overview of the subject, see Yonina Talmon, "Pursuit of the Millennium: The Relation Between Religious and Social Change," *Archives européennes de sociologie* III (1962): 125-48. One of the key classic works upon which much of the theory in this area is based is Ernst Troeltsch, *The Social Teaching of the Christian Churches,* trans. Olive Wyon, 2 vols. (New York: Macmillan, 1931). Troeltsch's theory is based on the work of his mentor, Max Weber, outlined in *The Protestant Ethic and the Spirit of Capitalism,* trans. Talcott Parsons, foreword by R. H. Tawney (New York: Charles Scribner's Sons, 1958). For an excellent summary by an evangelical of Troeltsch's theory and subsequent modifications made to it by other scholars, see David O. Moberg, *The Church as a Social Institution: The Sociology of American Religion* (Grand Rapids, Mich.: Baker, 1984), pp. 73-99.

[12]Norman Cohn, *The Pursuit of the Millennium* (New York: Oxford University Press, 1977), pp. 25-26; Michael J. St. Clair, *Millenarian Movements in Historical Context* (New York: Garland, 1992), pp. 79-85; "Montanism," in *The New International Dictionary of the Christian Church,* rev. ed. (Grand Rapids, Mich.: Zondervan, 1978).

[13]Paul Boyer, *When Time Shall Be No More: Prophecy Belief in Modern American Culture* (Cambridge: Belknap Press of Harvard University Press, 1992), pp. 48-49; Cohn, *Pursuit of the Millennium,* p. 29; St. Clair, *Millenarian Movements,* p. 87.

[14]Boyer, *When Time Shall Be No More,* pp. 52-53; Cohn, *Pursuit of the Millennium,* pp. 108-13; St. Clair, *Millenarian Movements,* pp. 99-101.

[15]St. Clair, *Millenarian Movements,* pp. 156-57.

[16]Gordon Rupp, *Patterns of Reformation* (London: Epworth, 1969), pp. 157-62; St. Clair, *Millenarian Movements,* pp. 156-58, 162; George Huntston Williams, *The Radical Reformation* (London: Weidenfeld and Nicolson, 1962), pp. 44-45.

[17]Rupp, *Reformation,* pp. 163-66; St. Clair, *Millenarian Movements,* pp. 128-31,

157-59; Williams, *Radical Reformation,* pp. 46-48.

[18]Thomas Müntzer, "Sermon Before the Princes," in *Spiritual and Anabaptist Writers: Documents Illustrative of the Radical Reformation,* ed. George Huntston Williams, Library of Christian Classics, vol. 25 (Philadelphia: Westminster, 1957), pp. 47-70; Rupp, *Reformation,* pp. 231-35; St. Clair, *Millenarian Movements,* pp. 159-65; Williams, *Radical Reformation,* pp. 53-55, 59-84.

[19]Rupp, *Reformation,* pp. 243-47; St. Clair, *Millenarian Movements,* pp. 166-67; Williams, *Radical Reformation,* pp. 77-78.

[20]St. Clair, *Millenarian Movements,* pp. 153-55, 172-84; Williams, *Radical Reformation,* pp. 368-81.

[21]William Miller, *Apology and Defense,* pp. 11-12, quoted in Francis D. Nichol, *The Midnight Cry* (Washington, D.C.: Review and Herald Publishing Association, 1945), p. 33. The title of Nichol's work was the battle cry of Millerites and reflected the urgency of their calling: proclaiming to the world Christ's imminent return. The phrase is taken from Jesus' parable of the ten virgins: "At midnight the cry rang out: 'Here's the bridegroom! Come out to meet him!' " (Mt 25:6; NASB). The book's subtitle, *A Defense of the Character and Conduct of William Miller and the Millerites, Who Mistakenly Believed that the Second Coming of Christ Would Take Place in the Year 1844,* may reveal Nichol's prejudice regarding his subject—he was, after all, a Seventh-day Adventist pastor. Nichol sought to defend the Millerites against the sensational accusations leveled at them, some of which appeared in the work on the Millerites that Nichol was responding to: Clara Endicott Sears, *Days of Delusion: A Strange Bit of History* (Boston: Houghton, Mifflin, 1924). Nevertheless, Nichol's book is still considered by scholars a balanced treatment and the most thorough—and thoroughly researched—single history of the Millerite movement. We use *The Midnight Cry* as the primary source for the Millerite narrative. (Nichol's work should be distinguished from the Millerite newspaper of the same name.)

[22]Nichol, *The Midnight Cry,* pp. 31-33.

[23]Ibid., pp. 441-43; J. F. C. Harrison, *The Second Coming: Popular Millenarianism, 1780-1850* (New Brunswick, N.J.: Rutgers University Press, 1979), pp. 193-94; "The Adventist Family," in *The Encyclopedia of American Religions,* 2 vols. (Wilmington, N.C.: McGrath, 1978), 1:460.

[24]Nichol, *The Midnight Cry,* pp. 34-35, 41-42.

[25]Ibid., pp. 43-53.

[26]Ibid., pp. 51-70.

[27]Ibid., pp. 71-84. For an extensive discussion of Himes and his role in the Millerite movement, see David T. Arthur, "Joshua V. Himes and the Cause of Adventism," in *The Disappointed: Millerism and Millenarianism in the Nineteenth Century* (Bloomington: Indiana University Press, 1987), pp. 36-58.

[28]Ibid., pp. 101-2, 104-13; Letter from L. C. Collins to Himes and Josiah Litch, May

23, 1842, in *Signs of the Times,* June 1, 1842, p. 69 (emphasis in the original), quoted in Nichol, *The Midnight Cry,* p. 103.

[29] *Signs of the Times,* July 13, 1842, pp. 114, 116, quoted in Nichol, *The Midnight Cry,* pp. 106, 121.

[30] Nichol, *The Midnight Cry,* pp. 126-30.

[31] Ibid., pp. 141, 157.

[32] *Signs of the Times,* Jan. 31, 1844, p. 195, quoted in Nichol, *The Midnight Cry,* p. 160.

[33] In the literature on the subject, the estimates for the number of Millerites range from thirty thousand to one million. For citations of 30,000, 40,000 and 100,000 Millerites, see Everett N. Dick, "The Millerite Movement, 1830-1845," in *Adventism in America,* ed. Gary Land (Grand Rapids, Mich.: Eerdmans, 1986), p. 34. For the estimate of one million Millerites, see Whitney R. Cross, *The Burned-over District: The Social and Intellectual History of Enthusiastic Religion in Western New York, 1800-1850* (Ithaca, N.Y.: Cornell University Press, 1950), p. 287. Cross cites Nichol, *The Midnight Cry,* p. 204, who quotes Miller himself claiming the movement had "fifty thousand believers," and Sears, *Days of Delusion,* p. 244, who states that "genuine" Millerites numbered fifty thousand but that countless nominal members greatly increased those numbers. It is difficult to know how Cross arrived at his estimate of one million.

[34] Dick, "Millerite Movement," p. 34.

[35] Nichol, *The Midnight Cry,* pp. 82-83.

[36] *Signs of the Times,* Feb. 22, 1843, p. 180, quoted in Nichol, *The Midnight Cry,* pp. 132-33.

[37] *First Report of the General Conference,* pp. 21-22, quoted in David T. Arthur, "Millerism," in *The Rise of Adventism: Religion and Society in Mid-Nineteenth-Century America,* ed. Edwin S. Gaustad (New York: Harper & Row, 1974), p. 157.

[38] Dick, "Millerite Movement," p. 34.

[39] See Cross, *Burned-over District,* and Barkun, *Crucible of the Millennium,* for extensive treatments of this theme.

[40] *Signs of the Times,* Feb. 22, 1843, p. 180, quoted in Nichol, *The Midnight Cry,* pp. 132-33.

[41] Nichol, *The Midnight Cry,* pp. 82, 91-95.

[42] *New York Herald Extra,* quoted in Nichol, *The Midnight Cry,* p. 122.

[43] Barkun, *Crucible of the Millennium,* pp. 49-52; *Signs of the Times,* Feb. 1, 1841, p. 162 (emphasis in the original), quoted in Barkun, *Crucible of the Millennium,* p. 52.

[44] Barkun, *Crucible of the Millennium,* pp. 50-54.

[45] Ibid., pp. 56-57; *Midnight Cry,* March 10, 1843, quoted in Barkun, *Crucible of the Millennium,* pp. 56.

[46] *The Liberator,* Feb. 17, 1843, p. 27 (emphasis in the original), quoted in Barkun, *Crucible of the Millennium,* p. 57.

[47]Barkun, *Crucible of the Millennium,* pp. 103-12.

[48]Ibid., pp. 113-23.

[49]Ibid.

[50]Nichol, *The Midnight Cry,* pp. 146-49; Barkun, *Crucible of the Millennium,* p. 40.

[51]Arthur, "Millerism," pp. 170-71.

[52]Ronald D. Graybill, "The Abolitionist-Millerite Connection," in *The Disappointed: Millerism and Millenarianism in the Nineteenth Century* (Bloomington: Indiana University Press, 1987), pp. 139-43. For an analysis of evangelicals and their role in the social issues of that time, see Timothy L. Smith, *Revivalism and Social Reform: American Protestantism on the Eve of the Civil War* (Gloucester, Mass.: Peter Smith, 1976).

[53]Letter from Silas Hawley, Aug. 15, 1843, in *Midnight Cry,* Aug. 24, 1843, p. 7, quoted in Nichol, *The Midnight Cry,* p. 147.

[54]*The Second Advent of Christ,* July 26, 1843, p. 2 (emphasis in the original), quoted in Nichol, *The Midnight Cry,* p. 148.

[55]Nichol, *The Midnight Cry,* pp. 152-53; Barkun, *Crucible of the Millennium,* p. 39.

[56]Nichol, *The Midnight Cry,* pp. 163-65.

[57]Ibid., pp. 165-66.

[58]Ibid., pp. 166-67; Arthur, "Millerism," pp. 169-71.

[59]Nichol, *The Midnight Cry,* pp. 169-73, 206-11.

[60]*Advent Herald,* March 20, 1844, p. 53, quoted in Nichol, *The Midnight Cry,* p. 207.

[61]Letter from Himes, Aug. 29, 1844, in *Midnight Cry,* Sept. 12, 1844, p. 80 (emphasis in the original), quoted in Nichol, *The Midnight Cry,* p. 212.

[62]Charles Fitch, *Come Out of Her, My People* (Rochester, N.Y.: J. V. Himes, 1843), p. 15, quoted in Arthur, "Millerism," p. 166. See Arthur, "Millerism," pp. 165-68, for a full discussion of the ramifications of Fitch's position.

[63]Nichol, *The Midnight Cry,* p. 212.

[64]Yonina Talmon, "Pursuit of the Millennium," pp. 125-48.

[65]Ibid., pp. 136-37. See also David Aberle, "A Note on Relative Deprivation Theory As Applied to Millenarian and Other Cult Movements," in *Millennial Dreams in Action: Studies in Revolutionary Religious Movements,* ed. Sylvia L. Thrupp (New York: Schocken Books, 1970), pp. 209-14.

[66]Talmon, "Pursuit of the Millennium," pp. 137-38.

[67]Ibid., p. 138.

[68]Charles Krauthammer, "The End of the World: Varieties of Apocalyptic Experience," *New Republic,* March 28, 1983, p. 15.

Chapter 5: The Results of Obsession

[1]*Signs of the Times,* Jan. 31, 1844, p. 195, quoted in Francis D. Nichol, *The Midnight Cry* (Washington, D.C.: Review and Herald Publishing Association, 1945), p. 158.

[2]Leon Festinger, Henry W. Riecken and Stanley Schachter, *When Prophecy Fails*

(Minneapolis: University of Minnesota Press, 1956), p. 3.

[3]Leon Festinger, *A Theory of Cognitive Dissonance* (Stanford, Calif.: Stanford University Press, 1957), pp. 1-3.

[4]Festinger et al., *When Prophecy Fails*, p. 3.

[5]Ibid., p. 4.

[6]Ibid.

[7]Ibid., pp. 4-5.

[8]Ibid., pp. 6-8; Michael J. St. Clair, *Millenarian Movements in Historical Context* (New York: Garland, 1992), pp. 170-74.

[9]Festinger et al., *When Prophecy Fails*, p. 29. Festinger states that although the Millerites offer an excellent demonstration of cognitive dissonance, the movement obviously cannot be observed firsthand now, and, therefore, a formal empirical study cannot be done. He hoped to produce such a study in *When Prophecy Fails*, a detailed analysis of a millenarian UFO cult. Because of the bizarre nature of that group, we felt it would have little bearing on our discussion, which is directed to evangelicals. Millerism, while not offering an exhaustive sociological study, is still the best-documented case of mainstream evangelical reaction to millennial fever and thus was chosen as the focus of our discussion.

[10]*Signs of the Times*, Jan. 25, 1843, p. 147, quoted in Nichol, *The Midnight Cry*, p. 126.

[11]Nichol, *The Midnight Cry*, pp. 141, 155-57, 210.

[12]Ibid., pp. 162-63.

[13]*Midnight Cry*, Feb. 15, 1844, p. 237, quoted in Nichol, *The Midnight Cry*, p. 163.

[14]*Advent Herald*, March 6, 1844, n.p., quoted in Nichol, *The Midnight Cry*, p. 162.

[15]Nichol, *The Midnight Cry*, pp. 169, 206.

[16]Ibid., pp. 170-71, 208. Sylvester Bliss, *Memoirs of William Miller* (Boston: J. V. Himes, 1853), p. 256 (emphasis in the original), quoted in Nichol, *The Midnight Cry*, p. 171.

[17]*Advent Herald*, July 17, 1844, p. 188, quoted in Nichol, *The Midnight Cry*, p. 208.

[18]Nichol, *The Midnight Cry*, pp. 208, 210.

[19]Ibid., pp. 207-8.

[20]Ibid., pp. 214, 229.

[21]Ibid., p. 216.

[22]*Midnight Cry*, Oct. 3, 1844, p. 104, quoted in Nichol, *The Midnight Cry*, p. 238.

[23]*Philadelphia Public Ledger*, Oct. 11, 1844, n.p., quoted in Nichol, *The Midnight Cry*, p. 239.

[24]Nichol, *The Midnight Cry*, pp. 239-40.

[25]Ibid., pp. 241-42, 370-72.

[26]*Advent Herald*, Oct. 16, 1844, n.p., quoted in Nichol, *The Midnight Cry*, p. 243.

[27]Nichol, *The Midnight Cry*, pp. 243-46.

[28]From Luther Boutelle, *Sketch of the Life and Religious Experience of Eld. Luther*

Boutelle (Boston: Advent Christian Publication Society, 1891), pp. 62-72, quoted in the appendix to Ronald L. Numbers and Jonathan M. Butler, eds., *The Disappointed: Millerism and Millenarianism in the Nineteenth Century,* (Bloomington: Indiana University Press, 1987), p. 211.

[29]Hiram Edson, undated manuscript fragment, Heritage Room, Andrews University Library, quoted in Numbers and Butler, eds., *The Disappointed,* p. 215.

[30]Dick, "Millerite Movement," p. 30.

[31]Ibid., p. 31; David L. Rowe, *Thunder and Trumpets: Millerites and Dissenting Religion in Upstate New York, 1800-1850* (Chico, Calif: Scholars Press, 1985), p. 142; Nichol, *Midnight Cry,* p. 251.

[32]Barkun, *Crucible of the Millennium,* p. 44.

[33]Letter from Miller to I. O. Orr, Dec. 13, 1844, quoted in Rowe, *Thunder and Trumpets,* p. 142.

[34]Rowe, *Thunder and Trumpets,* pp. 157-58.

[35]Ernest R. Sandeen, *The Roots of Fundamentalism: British and American Millenarianism, 1800-1930* (Chicago: University of Chicago Press, 1970), p. 58.

[36]For an extensive defense of Millerism regarding these issues, see Nichol, *The Midnight Cry,* pp. 337-69.

[37]Ronald L. Numbers and Janet S. Numbers, "Millerism and Madness: A Study of 'Religious Insanity' in Nineteenth-Century America," *Bulletin of the Menninger Clinic* 49 (1985): 297-301.

[38]Lawrence Foster, "Had Prophecy Failed? Contrasting Perspectives of the Millerites and Shakers," in *The Disappointed,* ed. Numbers and Butler, pp. 177, 181; Ruth Alden Doan, *The Miller Heresy, Millennialism, and American Culture* (Philadelphia: Temple University Press, 1987), p. 205.

[39]*Midnight Cry,* Dec. 5, 1844, n.p., quoted in Rowe, *Thunder and Trumpets,* p. 143.

[40]Dick, "Millerite Movement," p. 34.

[41]Rowe, *Thunder and Trumpets,* pp. 144-45.

[42]Ibid., pp. 145-49; Dick, "Millerite Movement," p. 32; Godfrey T. Anderson, "Sectarianism and Organization: 1846-1864," in *Adventism in America: A History,* ed. Gary Land (Grand Rapids, Mich.: Eerdmans, 1986), p. 39.

[43]Rowe, *Thunder and Trumpets,* pp. 152-55, 157-60.

[44]Land, ed., *Adventism in America,* p. vii.

[45]Anderson, "Sectarianism," p. 38; "The Adventist Family," p. 465.

[46]Anderson, "Sectarianism," p. 39; St. Clair, *Millenarian Movements,* p. 320.

[47]St. Clair, *Millenarian Movements,* pp. 320-21.

[48]Anderson, "Sectarianism," pp. 40-41.

[49]"The Adventist Family," p. 465; St. Clair, *Millenarian Movements,* pp. 321-24; Land, *Adventism in America,* pp. 241-50.

[50]The more detailed discussion of cognitive dissonance which follows is based on material in Festinger et al., *When Prophecy Fails,* pp. 25-30.

[51]Edgar C. Whisenant, *88 Reasons Why the Rapture Will Be in 1988* (Nashville: World Bible Society, 1988).

[52]Edgar C. Whisenant, *The Final Shout: Rapture Report 1989, 1990, 1991, 1992, 1993 . . .* (Nashville: World Bible Society, 1989), p. 1.

[53]Norvell L. Olive, opening letter to the reader, in Whisenant, *88 Reasons,* n.p.

[54]B. J. Oropeza, *99 Reasons Why No One Knows When Christ Will Return* (Downers Grove, Ill.: InterVarsity Press, 1994), pp. 88-89.

[55]For an excellent and exhaustive analysis of how Russia's role in biblical prophecy has been interpreted, see Dwight Wilson, *Armageddon Now! The Premillenarian Response to Russia and Israel Since 1917* (Grand Rapids, Mich.: Baker, 1977).

[56]Paul Boyer, *When Time Shall Be No More: Prophecy Beliefs in Modern American Culture* (Cambridge: Harvard University Press, 1992), pp. 325-31.

[57]Hal Lindsey, *Planet Earth—2000 A.D.: Will Mankind Survive?* (Palos Verdes, Calif.: Western Front, 1994), pp. 169-202.

[58]Ibid.; Hal Lindsey with C. C. Carlson, *The Late Great Planet Earth* (Grand Rapids: Zondervan, 1970), pp. 67-68, 146-68.

[59]Lindsey, *Planet Earth—2000 A.D.,* p. 191.

[60]Ibid., pp. 191-96 (emphasis in the original).

[61]Ibid., pp. 190-91.

[62]Kenneth Samples, Erwin de Castro, Richard Abanes and Robert Lyle, *Prophets of the Apocalypse: David Koresh and Other Messiahs* (Grand Rapids, Mich.: Baker, 1994), pp. 68-70.

[63]For a profile of life in the Waco compound, see Barbara Kantrowitz, "The Messiah of Waco," *Newsweek,* March 15, 1993, pp. 56-58.

[64]David Bunds, "Personal letter from David Bunds to Jaydee Wendell," n.d., quoted in Samples et al., *Prophets of the Apocalypse,* p. 69.

[65]Vernon W. Howell, "Personal Letter to the Seventh-day Adventist Church," n.d., quoted in Samples et al., *Prophets of the Apocalypse,* pp. 69-70.

[66]Samples et al., *Prophets of the Apocalypse,* pp. 77-96.

[67]Ibid., pp. 80-83.

[68]Ibid., pp. 83-84.

[69]Ibid., pp. 85-86; Nancy Gibbs, " 'Oh, My God, They're Killing Themselves!' " *Time,* May 3, 1993, p. 30.

[70]Samples et al., *Prophets of the Apocalypse,* p. 172.

[71]Michael Hirsley, "For World, It May Be the 9th Inning," *Chicago Tribune,* August 19, 1994, p. 2:9; David Briggs, Associated Press wire service story, July 13, 1994, n.p.; Joe Maxwell, "End-times Prediction Draws Strong Following," *Christianity Today,* June 20, 1994, pp. 46-47; Joe Maxwell, "Camping Misses End-times Deadline," *Christianity Today,* Oct. 24, 1994, p. 84. For a detailed critique of Camping's views, see Robert Sungenis, Scott Temple and David Allen Lewis, *Shock Wave 2000! The Harold Camping 1994 Debacle* (Green

Forest, Ark.: New Leaf, 1994) and Oropeza, *99 Reasons,* pp. 27, 31-32, 37-39, 43-44, 48-54, 57-61, 156.

[72]Hirsley, "For World, It May Be the 9th Inning," p. 2:9; Briggs, Associated Press wire service story, n.p.; Maxwell, "End-times Prediction Draws Strong Following," pp. 46-47; Maxwell, "Camping Misses End-times Deadline," p. 84.

[73]Maxwell, "Camping Misses End-times Deadline," p. 84.

Conclusion

[1]The pretribulationist rapture viewpoint (the belief that the return of Christ will take place in two stages—the rapture of the church before the Great Tribulation, after which the Second Coming of Christ in glory occurs) distinguishes itself here from the posttribulation viewpoint (the church will go through the Great Tribulation, after which occurs the Second Coming of Christ in glory). Technically, the former perspective does not anticipate the signs of the Second Coming, for it believes those events will not occur until the seven-year Great Tribulation period, after the rapture of the church. The latter perspective tends to emphasize the signs of the times.

[2]Oscar Cullmann, *Christ and Time: The Primitive Christian Conception of Time and History,* trans. Floyd V. Filson (Philadelphia: Westminster, 1950).

[3]For further discussion on this passage, see C. Marvin Pate, *The End of the Age Has Come: The Theology of Paul* (Grand Rapids, Mich.: Zondervan, 1994), pp. 85-87.

[4]See, in general, C. Marvin Pate, *The Glory of Adam and the Afflictions of the Righteous: Pauline Suffering in Context* (Lewiston, N.Y.: Edwin Mellen, 1993).

[5]Recall, for example, Dale C. Allison, *The End of the Ages Has Come: An Early Interpretation of the Passion and Resurrection of Jesus* (Philadelphia: Fortress, 1985). One need not conclude from this, however, that the church will go through the Great Tribulation; see Pate, *The End of the Age Has Come,* pp. 227-28.

[6]It is interesting to note that as far back as the Geneva Bible (1560) the footnote on Revelation 13:1-2 equates Pope Boniface with the antichrist. See Robert Fuller, *Naming the Antichrist: The History of an American Obsession* (New York: Oxford University Press, 1995) and Bernard McGinn, *Antichrist: Two Thousand Years of the Human Fascination with Evil* (San Francisco: HarperSanFrancisco, 1994) for full treatments of this phenomenon.

[7]Adam Clarke, *Commentary on the Whole Bible* (Grand Rapids, Mich.: Baker, 1967), p. 1058. Two of the best descriptions of this event are by Josephus (*Jewish War* 7:4-6) and Dio Cassius (*Roman History* 6).

[8]The phrase "principles *[stoicheia]* of the world" occurs three times in Paul's letters (Gal 4:3; Col 2:8, 20). Its meaning is contested, with three major possibilities surfacing: (1) principles such as an alphabet, elementary religious beliefs or mathematical propositions; (2) the four elements of the universe as enumerated in ancient Greek philosophy (earth, water, air and fire); (3) angelic beings that control the earth and astronomical bodies. Peter T. O'Brien in *Colossians, Philemon,* Word Biblical

Commentary 44 (Waco, Tex.: Word, 1982), pp. 129-32, provides a helpful overview of the issues involved and makes a convincing case for the third view.

[9]For further discussion on the defeat of the anti-God personages in the New Testament, see Pate, *The End of the Age Has Come,* pp. 45-54.

Selected Bibliography

Allison, Dale C. *The End of the Ages Has Come: An Early Interpretation of the Passion and Resurrection of Jesus*. Philadelphia: Fortress, 1985.

Anderson, Robert. *The Coming Prince*. 14th ed. Grand Rapids, Mich.: Kregel, 1954.

Aune, David E. *Prophecy in Early Christianity and the Ancient Mediterranean World*. Grand Rapids, Mich.: Eerdmans, 1983.

Barkun, Michael. *Crucible of the Millennium: The Burned-over District of New York in the 1840's*. Syracuse, N.Y.: Syracuse University Press, 1986.

Barrett, C. K. *The Gospel According to John*. 2nd ed. Philadelphia: Westminster, 1978.

Beagley, Alan James. *The "Sitz Im Leben" of the Apocalypse with Particular Reference to the Role of the Church's Enemies*. New York: Walter de Gruyter, 1987.

Beitzel, Barry J. *The Moody Atlas of Bible Lands*. Chicago: Moody Press, 1985.

Bliss, Sylvester. *Memoirs of William Miller*. Boston: J. V. Himes, 1853.

Boyer, Paul. *When Time Shall Be No More: Prophecy Beliefs in Modern American Culture*. Cambridge: Harvard University Press, 1992.

Campell, Donald K., and Jeffrey L. Townsend. *A Case for Premillennialism: A New Consensus*. Chicago: Moody Press, 1992.

Camping, Harold. *Are You Ready?* New York: Vantage, 1993.

———. *1994?* New York: Vantage, 1992.

Carrington, Philip. *The Meaning of Revelation*. London: SPCK, 1931.

Chandler, Russell. *Doomsday: The End of the World—A View Through Time*. Ann Arbor, Mich.: Servant Publications, 1993.

Charles, R. H. *A Critical and Exegetical Commentary on the Revelation of St. John*. 2 vols. International Critical Commentary. Edinburgh: T. & T. Clark, 1920.

Cohen, Daniel. *Waiting for the Apocalypse*. Buffalo, N.Y.: Prometheus, 1973.

Cohn, Norman. *The Pursuit of the Millennium*. New York: Oxford University Press, 1977.

Cranfield, C. E. B. *Romans IX—XVI*. International Critical Commentary. Edinburgh: T. & T. Clark, 1979.

Cross, Whitney R. *The Burned-over District: The Social and Intellectual History of Enthusiastic Religion in Western New York, 1800-1850*. Ithaca, N.Y.: Cornell University Press, 1950.

Doan, Ruth Alden. *The Miller Heresy, Millennialism, and American Culture*. Philadelphia: Temple University Press, 1987.

Dodd, C. H. *The Apostolic Preaching and Its Developments.* New York: Harper, 1944.

Fee, Gordon. *I and II Timothy, Titus.* Peabody, Mass.: Hendrickson, 1988.

Feinburg, John S., ed. *Continuity and Discontinuity: Perspectives on the Relationship Between the Old and New Testaments. Essays in Honor of S. Lewis Johnson, Jr.* Wheaton, Ill.: Crossway, 1988.

Ferguson, Everett. *Backgrounds of Early Christianity.* Grand Rapids, Mich.: Eerdmans, 1987.

Festinger, Leon. *A Theory of Cognitive Dissonance.* Stanford, Calif.: Stanford University Press, 1957.

Festinger, Leon, Henry W. Riecken and Stanley Schachter. *When Prophecy Fails.* Minneapolis: University of Minnesota Press, 1956.

Fitch, Charles. *Come Out of Her, My People.* Rochester, N.Y.: J. V. Himes, 1843.

Fitzmyer, Joseph A. *The Gospel According to Luke X—XXIV.* Anchor Bible Commentary, vol. 28A. New York: Doubleday, 1983.

Ford, J. Massyngberde. *Revelation.* Anchor Bible Commentary, vol. 39. New York: Doubleday, 1975.

Gaustad, Edwin S., ed. *The Rise of Adventism: Religion and Society in Mid-Nineteenth-Century America.* New York: Harper & Row, 1974.

Gentry, Kenneth L., Jr. *The Beast of Revelation.* Tyler, Tex.: Institute for Christian Economics, 1989.

———. *Before Jerusalem Fell: Dating the Book of Revelation.* Tyler, Tex.: Institute for Christian Economics, 1989.

Goldingay, John. *Daniel.* Word Biblical Commentary, vol. 30. Waco, Tex.: Word, 1989.

Gunkel, Herman. *Schöpfung und Chaos in Urzeit und Endzeit.* Göttingen: Vandenhoeck und Ruprecht, 1895.

Gurney, R. "The Four Kingdoms of Daniel 2 and 7." *Themelios* 2 (1977): 39-45.

Harrison, J. F. C. *The Second Coming: Popular Millenarianism, 1780-1850.* New Brunswick, N.J.: Rutgers University Press, 1979.

Horton, Michael S. *Beyond Culture Wars: Is America a Mission Field or a Battle Field?* Chicago: Moody Press, 1994.

Hunt, David. *Berean Call* newsletter. Bend, Ore.

Hunter, James Davison. *Before the Shooting Begins: Searching for Democracy in America's Culture War.* New York: Free Press, 1994.

———. *Culture Wars: The Struggle to Define America.* New York: Basic Books, 1991.

Jeffrey, Grant R. *Armageddon: Appointment with Destiny.* Toronto: Frontier Research, 1988.

Johnson, Alan F. "Revelation." In *Hebrews—Revelation.* Edited by Frank Gaebelein. Vol. 12 of *Expositors Bible Commentary.* Grand Rapids, Mich.: Zondervan, 1981.

Kalafian, Michael. *The Prophecy of the Seventy Weeks of the Book of Daniel.* Lanham,

Md.: University Press of America, 1991.

Kirban, Salem. *Countdown to Rapture.* Eugene, Ore.: Harvest House, 1977.

Lacocque, André. *The Book of Daniel.* Translated by David Pellauer. Atlanta: John Knox, 1979.

Ladd, George. "Apocalyptic." *Baker's Dictionary of Theology,* edited by E. F. Harrison. Grand Rapids, Mich.: Baker, 1960.

————. "Why Not Prophetic-Apocalyptic?" *Journal of Biblical Literature* 76 (1957): 192-200.

Land, Gary, ed. *Adventism in America: A History.* Grand Rapids, Mich.: Eerdmans, 1986.

Lindsey, Hal. *Planet Earth—2000 A.D.: Will Mankind Survive?* Palos Verdes, Calif.: Western Front, 1994.

Lindsey, Hal, with C. C. Carlson. *The Late Great Planet Earth.* Grand Rapids, Mich.: Zondervan, 1970.

Livingston, E. A. *Papers on the Gospels. Journal for the Study of the New Testament* Supplement Series. 2nd ed. Sheffield, U.K.: JSOT, 1980.

Longenecker, Richard. *Biblical Exegesis in the Apostolic Period.* Grand Rapids, Mich.: Eerdmans, 1975.

Malgo, Wim. *Israel's God Does Not Lie.* Hamilton, Ohio: Midnight Call, 1974.

————. *There Shall Be Signs in Heaven and on Earth.* Columbia, S.C.: Midnight Call, 1980.

Marsden, George M. *Fundamentalism and American Culture: The Shaping of Twentieth-Century Evangelicalism, 1870-1925.* Oxford: Oxford University Press, 1980.

————. *Understanding Fundamentalism and Evangelicalism.* Grand Rapids, Mich.: Eerdmans, 1991.

McGrath, Alister. *Evangelicalism and the Future of Christianity.* Downers Grove, Ill.: InterVarsity Press, 1995.

McKeever, James. *End-Times News Digest.* Medford, Ore.

Moberg, David O. *The Church as a Social Institution: The Sociology of American Religion.* Grand Rapids, Mich.: Baker, 1984.

Montgomery, J. A. *A Critical and Exegetical Commentary on the Book of Daniel.* Edinburgh: T. & T. Clark, 1927.

Moore, A. L. *The Parousia in the New Testament.* Leiden: E. J. Brill, 1966.

Morris, Leon. *Apocalyptic.* Grand Rapids, Mich.: Eerdmans, 1972.

Mounce, Robert H. *The Book of Revelation.* New International Commentary on the New Testament. Grand Rapids, Mich.: Eerdmans, 1977.

Müntzer, Thomas. "Sermon Before the Princes." In *Spiritual and Anabaptist Writers: Documents Illustrative of the Radical Reformation,* edited by George Huntston Williams. Library of Christian Classics, vol. 25. Philadelphia: Westminster, 1957.

Nichol, Francis D. *The Midnight Cry.* Washington, D.C.: Review and Herald Publishing Association, 1945.

Niebuhr, H. Richard. *The Social Sources of Denominationalism.* New York: Henry Holt, 1929.

Numbers, Ronald L., and Jonathan M. Butler, eds. *The Disappointed: Millerism and Millenarianism in the Nineteenth Century.* Bloomington: Indiana University Press, 1987.

Numbers, Ronald L., and Janet S. Numbers. "Millerism and Madness: A Study of 'Religious Insanity' in Nineteenth-Century America." *Bulletin of the Menninger Clinic* 49, no. 4 (1985): 289-320.

Oropeza, B. J. *99 Reasons Why No One Knows When Christ Will Return.* Downers Grove, Ill.: InterVarsity Press, 1994.

Pate, C. Marvin. *The End of the Age Has Come: The Theology of Paul.* Grand Rapids, Mich.: Zondervan, 1994.

————. *The Glory of Adam and the Afflictions of the Righteous: Pauline Suffering in Context.* Lewiston, N.Y.: Edwin Mellen, 1993.

Payne, J. Barton. *Encyclopedia of Biblical Prophecy.* New York: Harper & Row, 1973.

Reeves, Marjorie. *The Influence of Prophecy in the Later Middle Ages: A Study in Joachism.* Oxford: Clarendon Press, 1969.

Relfe, Mary Stewart. *When Your Money Fails: The 666 System Is Here.* Montgomery, Ala.: Ministries, 1981.

Robertson, Pat. *The New Millennium.* Dallas: Word, 1990.

————. *The New World Order.* Dallas: Word, 1992.

Rowe, David L. *Thunder and Trumpets: Millerites and Dissenting Religion in Upstate New York, 1800-1850.* Chico, Calif.: Scholars, 1985.

Rowley, H. H. *Darius the Mede and the Four World Empires in the Book of Daniel.* Cardiff: University of Wales, 1959.

————. *The Relevance of Apocalyptic: A Study of Jewish and Christian Apocalypses from Daniel to Revelation.* London & Redhill: Lutterworth Press, 1947.

Rupp, Gordon. *Patterns of Reformation.* London: Epworth, 1969.

Russell, D. S. *Apocalyptic: Ancient and Modern.* Philadelphia: Fortress, 1978.

————. *The Method and Message of Jewish Apocalyptic.* Philadelphia: Westminster, 1964.

Ryrie, Charles. *Dispensationalism Today.* Chicago: Moody Press, 1965.

St. Clair, Michael J. *Millenarian Movements in Historical Context.* New York: Garland, 1992.

Samples, Kenneth, Erwin de Castro, Richard Abanes and Robert Lyle. *Prophets of the Apocalypse: David Koresh and Other American Messiahs.* Grand Rapids, Mich.: Baker, 1994.

Sandeen, Ernest R. *The Roots of Fundamentalism: British and American Millenarianism, 1800-1930.* Chicago: University of Chicago Press, 1970.

Schweizer, Eduard. *The Good News According to Matthew.* Translated by David E. Green. Atlanta: John Knox, 1975.

Sears, Clara Endicott. *Days of Delusion: A Strange Bit of History.* Boston: Houghton Mifflin, 1924.

Smith, Chuck. *Future Survival.* Costa Mesa, Calif.: Calvary Chapel, 1978.

Smith, Timothy L. *Revivalism and Social Reform: American Protestantism on the Eve of the Civil War.* Gloucester, Mass.: Peter Smith, 1976.

Sproston, Wendy E. *Satan in the Fourth Gospel. Studia Biblica 1978. II. Papers on the Gospels.* Journal for the Study of the New Testament Supplement Series 2. Edited by E. A. Livingstone. Sheffield: JSOT, 1980.

Talmon, Yonina. "Pursuit of the Millennium: The Relationship Between Religious and Social Change." *Archives européennes de sociologie* 3 (1962): 125-48.

Thrupp, Sylvia, ed. *Millennial Dreams in Action: Studies in Revolutionary Religious Movements.* New York: Schocken Books, 1970.

Troeltsch, Ernest. *The Social Teaching of the Christian Churches.* 2 vols. Translated by Olive Wyon. New York: Macmillan, 1931.

Virkler, Henry. *Hermeneutics: Principles and Processes of Biblical Interpretation.* Grand Rapids, Mich.: Baker, 1988.

Vos, Louis A. *The Synoptic Traditions in the Apocalypse.* Kampen, The Netherlands: Kok, 1965.

Walton, John H. "The Four Kingdoms of Daniel." *Journal of the Evangelical Theological Society* 29, no. 1 (1986).

Weber, Max. *The Protestant Ethic and the Spirit of Capitalism.* Translated by Talcott Parsons. New York: Charles Scribner's Sons, 1958.

Weber, Timothy P. *Living in the Shadow of the Second Coming: American Premillennialism 1875-1925.* New York: Oxford University Press.

Whisenant, Edgar C. *88 Reasons Why the Rapture Will Be in 1988.* Nashville: World Bible Society, 1988.

————. *The Final Shout: Rapture Report 1989, 1990, 1991, 1992, 1993 . . .* Nashville: World Bible Society, 1989.

Williams, George Huntston. *The Radical Reformation.* London: Weidenfeld and Nicolson, 1962.

Wilson, Bryan R. "An Analysis of Sect Development." *American Sociological Review* 24, no. 1 (1959): 3-15.

————. *Religion in Sociological Perspective.* New York: Oxford University Press, 1982.

————. *Sects and Society: A Sociological Study of Elim Tabernacle, Christian Science, and Christadelphians.* Berkeley: University of California Press, 1961.

Wilson, Dwight. *Armageddon Now! The Premillenarian Response to Russia and Israel since 1917.* Grand Rapids, Mich.: Baker, 1977.

Yamauchi, Edwin. *Foes from the Northern Frontier.* Grand Rapids, Mich.: Baker, 1982.